TEEN COOKBOOK

EFFORTLESSLY

Create delicious dishes stress-free! Step-by-step video recipes and easy-to-follow guides will help you become a confident, creative, and joyful chef.

Kila Frost

Contents

Chapter 1: Getting Started in the Kitchen

To kick off your culinary journey, the first step is to ensure you have all the necessary ingredients and tools at your disposal. This means creating a comprehensive shopping list that covers everything you'll need to whip up the delicious recipes featured in this book. From the basics for a Pancake Stack with Maple Syrup to the more exotic ingredients for a Mango Pineapple Smoothie, having the right items in your pantry and fridge will set you up for success. Here's a detailed shopping list to get you started:

- All-purpose flour (for pancakes, muffins, cookies, and more)
- Baking powder
- Baking soda
- Salt
- Granulated sugar
- Brown sugar
- Vanilla extract
- Eggs
- Milk (dairy or non-dairy alternatives)
- Butter
- Maple syrup
- Avocados
- Fresh berries (strawberries, blueberries, raspberries)
- Greek yogurt
- Granola
- Bananas
- Nuts (walnuts, almonds)
- Salsa
- Cinnamon
- Bread (whole grain, sourdough, or your choice)
- Oats
- Chocolate chips
- Cream cheese
- Heavy cream
- Cocoa powder

- Peanut butter
- Lemons
- Apples
- Strawberries
- Cream of tartar
- Coconut oil
- Olive oil
- Various cheeses (cheddar, mozzarella, parmesan, feta)
- Turkey breast slices
- Chicken breasts
- Shrimp
- Ground beef
- Pork shoulder
- Tortillas (flour or corn)
- Pasta (spaghetti, penne, ziti)
- Rice
- Fresh vegetables (lettuce, tomatoes, cucumbers, bell peppers, onions, garlic, zucchini, sweet potatoes, avocados, spinach)
- Fresh herbs (basil, parsley, cilantro)
- Canned tuna
- Capers
- Olives
- Pesto sauce
- BBQ sauce
- Soy sauce
- Teriyaki sauce

- Lemon juice
- Pineapple
- Mango
- Coconut milk
- Almond milk

- Green tea powder (matcha)
- Watermelon
- Peaches
- Mint leaves

Remember, this list is just the beginning. Feel free to add any additional spices, condiments, or ingredients you love to personalize your dishes. The key is to have fun and experiment in the kitchen, using this list as a foundation to build upon. With these items ready and waiting, you're all set to dive into the world of cooking, creating mouthwatering meals that will impress your family and friends.

Kitchen Basics

Once you've stocked your kitchen with the essential ingredients, the next step is to familiarize yourself with the tools and equipment that will transform those ingredients into delectable dishes. Every chef, no matter their age or experience level, needs a reliable set of tools to navigate the culinary world successfully. **Measuring cups and spoons** are indispensable for following recipes accurately, ensuring that your creations turn out just right every time. A set of **mixing bowls** in various sizes will serve multiple purposes, from mixing batter to tossing salads. **Knives** are the cornerstone of kitchen tools; a sharp chef's knife and a paring knife can handle most cutting tasks, from chopping vegetables to slicing meat. Don't forget a **cutting board**—preferably two, one for fresh produce and another for raw meats, to avoid cross-contamination.

Spatulas, wooden spoons, and whisks cover a wide range of cooking tasks, from flipping pancakes to stirring sauces. A **can opener** and a **vegetable peeler** are also essential for preparing ingredients. When it comes to cooking, a **set of pots and pans** is crucial. A large pot for soups and pasta, a saucepan for sauces and grains, and a frying pan for sautéing and frying will have you covered for most recipes. For baking, a set of **baking sheets and pans** in different shapes and sizes will allow you to experiment with everything from cookies to cakes to casseroles.

Understanding how to use these tools effectively is just as important as having them. For instance, knowing when to use a wooden spoon instead of a metal spatula can prevent your non-stick pans from getting scratched. Similarly, mastering knife skills can make prep work much quicker and safer. Start by learning how to hold a knife properly, keeping the tip of the knife on the cutting board and rocking it back and forth to slice through ingredients. Practice makes perfect, so don't be discouraged if you're slow at first. Speed and confidence will come with time and experience.

In addition to these basics, there are a few other gadgets and utensils that can make your cooking experience even more enjoyable. A **grater** for cheese and vegetables, a **zester** for adding citrus flavor to dishes, and **measuring scales** for precise ingredient measurements can elevate your cooking from good to great. While not strictly necessary, these tools can expand your culinary repertoire and inspire you to try new recipes.

A **blender** or **food processor** is another versatile tool that can be a game-changer in the kitchen, especially for making smoothies, soups, and sauces. It's a great way to incorporate fruits and vegetables into your diet in a fun and delicious way. Remember to always handle these appliances with care, ensuring they are properly assembled before use to avoid any accidents.

For those interested in baking, investing in a **stand mixer** or a **hand mixer** can significantly reduce the effort required for mixing doughs and batters. While mixing by hand can be a rewarding experience, these tools provide a level of consistency and efficiency that's hard to match. Plus, they open up the possibility of exploring more complex recipes that require precise mixing techniques.

Storage is another critical aspect of kitchen basics. Having a set of **airtight containers** allows you to store leftovers safely and keeps ingredients fresh longer. Labeling these containers with the contents and date ensures that you don't forget what you have, reducing waste and saving money in the long run.

Maintaining your tools and equipment is essential for their longevity and your safety. Regularly sharpen your knives to keep them cutting efficiently and safely. Clean your appliances after each use according to the manufacturer's instructions to prevent buildup and ensure they operate correctly. Non-stick pans should be washed with a soft sponge to avoid damaging the surface, while wooden utensils are best hand-washed to prevent cracking.

Finally, understanding the importance of **mise en place**, or having all your ingredients prepped and ready to go before you start cooking, can transform your cooking experience. It not only saves time but also reduces stress, allowing you to enjoy the process and focus on the techniques. This practice is especially useful in ensuring that you don't miss any steps or ingredients in a recipe.

By familiarizing yourself with these tools, techniques, and practices, you'll be well on your way to becoming a confident and joyful chef. Remember, the kitchen is a place for creativity and experimentation, so don't be afraid to try new things and make adjustments based on your preferences. With the right tools and a bit of practice, you'll be able to create delicious dishes that will impress anyone.

Essential Tools and Equipment

Beyond the basics, there are a few **specialized tools** that can elevate your cooking game and make certain tasks much easier. For example, a **microplane** is perfect for grating hard spices like nutmeg or zesting citrus fruits to add a burst of flavor to your dishes. A **silicone baking mat** can be a game-changer for baking, providing a non-stick surface that helps with even heat distribution and makes cleanup a breeze.

For those who love to bake, a **rolling pin** is essential for rolling out doughs for pies, cookies, and pizzas. Opt for one that feels comfortable in your hands, as you'll be applying pressure evenly across the dough. A **pastry brush** is another handy tool for applying egg washes, butter, or glazes to your baked goods, ensuring they come out of the oven with a beautiful, golden finish.

Digital kitchen scales offer precision that measuring cups can't match, especially for baking where exact measurements are crucial. They're also incredibly useful for portioning out servings, which can be a great skill to learn for meal prep or when cooking for friends and family.

A **thermometer** is a must-have for safely cooking meats and poultry to the correct internal temperature, ensuring that your dishes are both safe to eat and perfectly prepared. There are various types available, from instant-read to probe thermometers that can stay in the meat while it cooks in the oven.

For those interested in exploring international cuisines, a **mortar and pestle** can be used for grinding spices and making pastes, releasing their full flavor in a way that pre-ground spices can't match. Similarly, a **wok** is essential for authentic stir-frying, as its high sides and shape allow for quick cooking and easy tossing of ingredients.

Storage solutions also play a critical role in the kitchen. **Magnetic knife strips** keep knives safely stored and easily accessible, while **spice racks** or **drawer organizers** can help keep your spices and utensils organized and within reach. This not only helps in keeping your kitchen tidy but also saves time during cooking as you won't need to search through cluttered drawers.

For those who enjoy making pizzas or artisan bread, a **pizza stone** or **baking steel** can mimic the effects of a professional oven, giving you a crispy crust that's hard to achieve with a regular baking sheet. Similarly, a **dough scraper** can be invaluable for working with sticky doughs, helping to cut and shape them with ease.

Safety equipment should not be overlooked. A **fire extinguisher** specifically designed for kitchen use, **oven mitts** that provide ample protection, and **apron** to protect your clothes from splatters and spills are all important. Additionally, investing in a **first aid kit** tailored for minor kitchen injuries can provide peace of mind.

Each of these tools can open up new possibilities in the kitchen, allowing you to experiment with techniques and recipes that were previously out of reach. While not all of them are strictly necessary, selecting a few based on your interests and the types of dishes you enjoy making can enhance your cooking experience significantly. Remember, the goal is to equip yourself with tools that not only make cooking more efficient but also more enjoyable. As you grow more confident and skilled in the kitchen, you may find yourself drawn to even more specialized equipment, but these essentials will serve as the foundation of your culinary adventures.

Understanding Ingredients

Mastering the art of cooking begins with a deep understanding of ingredients, their flavors, and how they interact with each other. This knowledge is crucial for anyone looking to create dishes that are not only delicious but also balanced and harmonious. For novice chefs, especially teens venturing into the culinary world, grasping the basics of ingredients can transform cooking from a task into an exciting exploration of taste and creativity.

Ingredients can be categorized into several groups, each playing a unique role in the cooking process. **Proteins**, such as chicken, beef, tofu, and beans, are the building blocks of many meals, providing substance and satisfaction. Understanding the different cooking methods for each protein, like baking, grilling, or sautéing, can significantly impact the final dish's flavor and texture. For instance, marinating chicken in herbs and spices before grilling can infuse it with flavors that baking might not achieve.

Vegetables and fruits add color, texture, and vital nutrients to dishes. The freshness of these ingredients is paramount; fresh, in-season produce often offers the best taste and nutritional value. Learning to pair the right vegetables and fruits with your main protein can elevate a simple dish to something special. For example, the sweetness of roasted carrots or the tartness of fresh berries can complement the richness of meats or the creaminess of dairy-based sauces.

Carbohydrates, including pasta, rice, and bread, serve as the energy component of a meal. The key with carbohydrates is understanding their cooking times and what textures they bring to a dish. Al dente pasta, fluffy rice, and crusty bread can each transform a meal's complexity and satisfaction level.

Fats and oils, such as butter, olive oil, and avocado, are essential for cooking and flavoring. They can carry and amplify flavors from herbs and spices, add moisture to dishes, and provide a satisfying mouthfeel. Knowing when to use a particular type of fat—like olive oil for dressings and butter for baking—can make a significant difference in your cooking.

Herbs and spices are the magic ingredients that can transport a dish from mundane to extraordinary. Fresh herbs like basil, cilantro, and parsley add a burst of freshness, while dried spices like cumin, paprika, and cinnamon introduce depth and warmth. Experimenting with these can be one of the most enjoyable aspects of cooking, as you learn how different flavors complement or contrast with each other.

Understanding the concept of **seasoning** is also crucial. Salt is more than just a flavor enhancer; it can alter the structure of proteins, making them juicier, and help balance sweetness or acidity in a dish.

Learning to season correctly, which often means tasting and adjusting throughout the cooking process, is a skill that will significantly improve the quality of your dishes.

Another essential aspect of ingredients is their **storage**. Proper storage can extend the life of your ingredients and preserve their quality. For example, storing herbs in a glass of water in the refrigerator can keep them fresh longer, while keeping nuts and seeds in the freezer can prevent them from going rancid.

Lastly, the concept of **substitutions** offers flexibility and creativity in cooking. Whether due to dietary restrictions, allergies, or simply lacking an ingredient, knowing how to substitute without compromising the dish's integrity is a valuable skill. For instance, using Greek yogurt as a substitute for sour cream in recipes can maintain the creamy texture while offering a healthier alternative.

By gaining a comprehensive understanding of ingredients and their roles in cooking, you'll be able to make informed decisions that enhance your dishes. This knowledge not only makes the cooking process more enjoyable but also allows for greater creativity and experimentation in the kitchen. As you continue to explore and learn, remember that cooking is as much about intuition and personal taste as it is about technique and precision.

Safety and Hygiene

Maintaining a clean and safe kitchen is paramount, especially for novice chefs. **Safety and hygiene** in the kitchen encompass a range of practices, from proper food handling to the cleanliness of your cooking space. Here are essential guidelines to ensure your kitchen remains a safe environment for cooking:

1. **Wash Your Hands** - Always wash your hands with soap and warm water before and after handling food, particularly raw meats, poultry, and seafood. This simple act can prevent the spread of harmful bacteria and viruses.

2. **Keep Surfaces Clean** - Regularly clean countertops, cutting boards, and appliances with hot, soapy water. After preparing raw meat, it's crucial to disinfect these surfaces to avoid cross-contamination.

3. **Separate Raw and Cooked Foods** - Use separate cutting boards and utensils for raw meats and other ingredients. This practice helps prevent bacteria from raw foods contaminating cooked or ready-to-eat foods.

4. **Cook Foods to Safe Temperatures** - Use a food thermometer to ensure meats, poultry, and fish are cooked to the temperatures recommended by food safety guidelines. This is the only reliable way to ensure harmful bacteria are killed.

5. **Store Foods Properly** - Refrigerate or freeze perishable foods promptly. Understand the importance of keeping cold foods cold and hot foods hot to inhibit bacterial growth. Be mindful of expiration dates and storage recommendations on food packaging.

6. **Avoid Cross-Contamination** - Keep raw meat, poultry, seafood, and their juices away from other foods in your refrigerator. Consider storing these items in a separate bin or on the lowest shelf to prevent drips onto other foods.

7. **Thaw Foods Safely** - Never thaw foods at room temperature. Instead, thaw foods in the refrigerator, in cold water (changing the water every 30 minutes), or in the microwave if you plan to cook them immediately afterward.

8. **Use Clean Dishcloths and Sponges** - Dishcloths and sponges can harbor bacteria. Wash them regularly in hot water or the washing machine, and replace sponges frequently. Consider using paper towels for cleaning surfaces that have come into contact with raw meat.

9. **Dress Appropriately** - Tie back long hair and avoid loose clothing that could catch fire or get caught in appliances. Wear closed-toe shoes to protect your feet from spills and dropped kitchen tools.

10. **Handle Knives Carefully** - Learn proper knife handling and cutting techniques to prevent injuries. Always cut away from your body, keep knives sharp, and store them safely in a block or on a magnetic strip.

11. **Be Prepared for Emergencies** - Keep a first-aid kit, fire extinguisher, and baking soda (for extinguishing grease fires) easily accessible in the kitchen. Know basic first aid and how to use a fire extinguisher.

12. **Dispose of Waste Properly** - Regularly take out the trash to avoid attracting pests. Use a compost bin for vegetable scraps if possible, and ensure it's emptied and cleaned regularly.

13. **Mind Electrical Safety** - Keep electrical appliances away from wet areas and never handle them with wet hands. Unplug appliances when not in use, especially those with blades or heating elements.

14. **Stay Organized** - A cluttered kitchen can lead to accidents. Keep the cooking area clear, and store tools and ingredients properly when not in use. This not only makes cooking more efficient but also safer.

By adhering to these safety and hygiene practices, you'll create a kitchen environment that's not only conducive to learning and creativity but also minimizes the risk of accidents and foodborne illnesses. Remember, a safe chef is a successful chef.

Chapter 2: 10 Breakfast Recipes

Pancake Stack with Maple Syrup

Difficulty Level: ★☆☆☆☆

Total Time: 30 minutes

Servings: 4

Ingredients:

- 1 cup all-purpose flour
- 2 tablespoons sugar
- 1 tablespoon baking powder
- 1/2 teaspoon salt
- 1 cup milk
- 2 tablespoons unsalted butter, melted, plus more for cooking
- 1 large egg
- 1 teaspoon vanilla extract
- Maple syrup, for serving
- Fresh berries (optional), for serving

Required Equipment:

- Mixing bowls
- Whisk
- Measuring cups and spoons
- Non-stick skillet or griddle
- Spatula

Preparation:

1. In a large mixing bowl, whisk together the flour, sugar, baking powder, and salt.
2. In another bowl, beat the milk, melted butter, egg, and vanilla extract until well combined.
3. Pour the wet ingredients into the dry ingredients. Stir until just combined; it's okay if the batter is a bit lumpy.
4. Heat a non-stick skillet or griddle over medium heat and brush with a little melted butter.

5. Pour 1/4 cup of batter onto the skillet for each pancake. Cook until bubbles form on the surface, then flip with a spatula and cook until golden brown on the other side, about 2 minutes per side.

6. Serve the pancakes hot with maple syrup and, if desired, fresh berries on top.

Chef's Tip:

- For fluffier pancakes, let the batter sit for 5-10 minutes before cooking. This allows the baking powder to activate.
- Experiment with add-ins like chocolate chips or sliced bananas by folding them into the batter before cooking.
- If you're using a griddle, you can cook multiple pancakes at once, which is great for serving a crowd.

Nutritional Information per Serving:

- Calories: 250
- Fat: 8g
- Carbohydrates: 38g
- Protein: 6g
- Sugar: 10g
- Sodium: 480mg

(Note: Nutritional values are approximate and can vary based on ingredient brands and serving sizes.)

Avocado Toast with Poached Egg

Difficulty Level: ★★☆☆☆

Total Time: 20 minutes

Servings: 2

Ingredients:
- 1 ripe avocado
- 2 large eggs
- 2 slices of whole grain bread
- 1 tablespoon white vinegar
- Salt and pepper to taste
- Optional toppings: red pepper flakes, chopped cilantro, or a squeeze of lemon juice

Required Equipment:
- Pot for boiling water

- Slotted spoon
- Toaster
- Knife
- Fork

Preparation:

1. Fill a pot with about 3 inches of water and add the white vinegar. Bring the water to a simmer over medium heat.

2. Crack each egg into a small bowl or cup. Once the water is simmering, gently slide the eggs into the water one at a time. Cook for 3 to 4 minutes for a soft poached egg or 4 to 5 minutes for a firmer yolk.

3. While the eggs are poaching, toast the bread slices to your desired level of crispiness.

4. Cut the avocado in half, remove the pit, and scoop the flesh into a bowl. Mash the avocado with a fork until it reaches your preferred consistency. Season with salt and pepper.

5. Spread the mashed avocado evenly onto the toasted bread slices.

6. Using the slotted spoon, carefully remove the poached eggs from the water and drain them on a paper towel to remove any excess water.

7. Place a poached egg on top of each avocado toast. Add any optional toppings you like.

8. Season with additional salt and pepper to taste.

Chef's Tip:

- For an extra kick, sprinkle your avocado toast with red pepper flakes or drizzle with a bit of olive oil.
- If you're not confident about poaching eggs, you can also try a fried or soft-boiled egg as a simpler alternative.

Nutritional Information per Serving:
- Calories: 300
- Protein: 12g
- Fat: 20g
- Carbohydrates: 22g
- Fiber: 7g
- Sugar: 3g

Berry Smoothie Bowl

Difficulty Level: ★☆☆☆☆

Total Time: 10 minutes

Servings: 2

Ingredients:

- 1 cup frozen mixed berries (strawberries, blueberries, raspberries)
- 1 frozen banana, sliced
- 1/2 cup Greek yogurt
- 1/2 cup almond milk (or any milk of your choice)
- 1 tablespoon honey (optional)
- Toppings: Sliced fresh fruits (banana, strawberries, kiwi), granola, coconut flakes, chia seeds, nuts

Required Equipment:

- Blender
- Measuring cups and spoons
- Two serving bowls
- Spoon for mixing toppings

Preparation:

1. Place the frozen mixed berries, frozen banana slices, Greek yogurt, almond milk, and honey (if using) into the blender.
2. Blend on high speed until the mixture is smooth and creamy. If the smoothie is too thick, you can add a little more milk to reach your desired consistency.
3. Pour the smoothie mixture evenly into two serving bowls.
4. Decorate the top of each smoothie bowl with your chosen toppings. Arrange sliced fruits, sprinkle granola, coconut flakes, chia seeds, and nuts according to your preference.
5. Serve immediately and enjoy your colorful, nutritious breakfast!

Chef's Tip:

- For an extra protein boost, add a scoop of your favorite protein powder to the blender before mixing.
- Feel free to get creative with the toppings! The more color and texture, the better.
- If you prefer your smoothie bowl to be a bit sweeter, you can add more honey or a splash of maple syrup.

Nutritional Information per Serving:

- Calories: Approximately 300 (varies with toppings)
- Protein: 10g
- Carbohydrates: 55g
- Fat: 5g
- Fiber: 8g
- Sugar: 30g (Natural sugars from fruits)

Classic French Omelette

Difficulty Level: ★☆☆☆☆

Total Time: 15 minutes

Servings: 1

Ingredients:
- 3 large eggs
- 1 tablespoon unsalted butter
- Salt, to taste
- Pepper, to taste
- Optional fillings: cheese, herbs, diced ham, sautéed mushrooms

Required Equipment:
- Non-stick skillet (8-inch)
- Whisk or fork
- Spatula
- Mixing bowl

Preparation:

1. Crack the eggs into a mixing bowl. Add a pinch of salt and pepper. Whisk the eggs vigorously until the mixture is uniform in color and slightly frothy.

2. Heat the non-stick skillet over medium-low heat. Add the butter and let it melt completely, swirling the skillet to coat the bottom evenly.

3. Once the butter is fully melted and starts to bubble slightly, pour the whisked eggs into the skillet. Let the eggs sit undisturbed for about 30 seconds, allowing the bottom to start setting.

4. With the spatula, gently stir the eggs, pushing them from the edges towards the center. Tilt the skillet as needed to allow the uncooked eggs to flow to the edges and set.

5. When the eggs are mostly set but still slightly runny on top, add any optional fillings across the center of the omelette.

6. Carefully fold one side of the omelette over the fillings towards the center, then fold the other side over to enclose the fillings completely.

7. Let the omelette cook for another 30 seconds to ensure it's fully set and the fillings are warmed through.

8. Gently slide the omelette onto a plate. Serve immediately.

Chef's Tip:

- For a fluffy omelette, add a splash of milk or cream to the eggs before whisking.
- Experiment with different fillings to find your favorite combinations. Just remember to cook any raw ingredients, like mushrooms or onions, before adding them to the omelette.
- If you're having trouble flipping or folding the omelette, use a plate to help flip it over in the skillet, then slide it back in to finish cooking.

Nutritional Information per Serving:

- Calories: 220 (without fillings)
- Protein: 18g
- Fat: 16g
- Carbohydrates: 1g
- Sodium: 210mg
- Cholesterol: 555mg

Banana Nut Muffins

Difficulty Level: ★☆☆☆☆

Total Time: 30 minutes

Servings: 12 muffins

Ingredients:

- 1 1/2 cups all-purpose flour
- 1 teaspoon baking soda
- 1 teaspoon baking powder
- 1/2 teaspoon salt
- 3 ripe bananas, mashed
- 3/4 cup sugar
- 1 egg, lightly beaten
- 1/3 cup unsalted butter, melted
- 1/2 cup walnuts, chopped

Required Equipment:

- Muffin tin

- 12 paper muffin liners
- Mixing bowls
- Fork
- Whisk
- Spoon or ice cream scoop

Preparation:

1. Preheat your oven to 375°F (190°C). Line a muffin tin with paper liners.

2. In a large bowl, whisk together the flour, baking soda, baking powder, and salt.

3. In another bowl, mix the mashed bananas, sugar, egg, and melted butter until well combined.

4. Pour the banana mixture into the dry ingredients. Use a fork to blend everything together until moistened. Do not overmix; the batter should be slightly lumpy.

5. Gently fold in the chopped walnuts.

6. Use a spoon or an ice cream scoop to fill the muffin liners about three-quarters full with batter.

7. Bake in the preheated oven for 18-20 minutes, or until a toothpick inserted into the center of a muffin comes out clean.

8. Allow the muffins to cool in the pan for 5 minutes, then transfer them to a wire rack to cool completely.

Chef's Tip:

- For an extra touch of sweetness and texture, sprinkle a little brown sugar and a few chopped walnuts on top of each muffin before baking.
- If you prefer your muffins a bit more moist, add an extra banana to the batter.
- These muffins freeze well. Just wrap them individually in plastic wrap and freeze. Thaw and reheat in the microwave for a quick breakfast or snack.

Nutritional Information per Serving:

- Calories: 210
- Fat: 8g
- Saturated Fat: 3.5g
- Cholesterol: 25mg
- Sodium: 220mg
- Carbohydrates: 32g
- Fiber: 1g
- Sugar: 17g
- Protein: 3g

Breakfast Burrito with Salsa

Difficulty Level: ★★☆☆☆

Total Time: 30 minutes

Servings: 4

Ingredients:

- 4 large eggs
- 1/4 cup milk
- Salt and pepper, to taste
- 1 tablespoon olive oil
- 4 large flour tortillas
- 1 cup shredded cheddar cheese
- 1 cup cooked and crumbled breakfast sausage
- 1 ripe avocado, sliced
- 1/2 cup fresh salsa

Required Equipment:

- Non-stick skillet
- Mixing bowl
- Whisk
- Spatula
- Microwave or stovetop (for warming tortillas)

Preparation:

1. In a mixing bowl, whisk together eggs, milk, salt, and pepper until well combined.
2. Heat olive oil in a non-stick skillet over medium heat. Pour in the egg mixture and cook, stirring occasionally, until the eggs are scrambled and fully cooked, about 3-4 minutes. Remove from heat.
3. Warm the flour tortillas on a stovetop or in the microwave until they are soft and pliable.
4. Lay out the warmed tortillas on a flat surface. Divide the scrambled eggs evenly among the tortillas, placing them in the center.
5. Top the eggs with shredded cheddar cheese, crumbled breakfast sausage, and sliced avocado.
6. Spoon fresh salsa over the top of the fillings.
7. Fold the bottom edge of the tortilla up over the fillings, then fold in the sides and roll up tightly.
8. Serve immediately, with additional salsa on the side if desired.

Chef's Tip:

- For a vegetarian option, replace the breakfast sausage with black beans or sautéed vegetables.
- Customize your breakfast burrito with additional toppings like sour cream, hot sauce, or diced tomatoes for extra flavor.
- If you prefer a crispy outer shell, after rolling the burritos, place them back in the skillet over medium heat for 1-2 minutes on each side until golden brown.

Nutritional Information per Serving:

- Calories: 450
- Protein: 22g
- Carbohydrates: 35g
- Fat: 25g
- Sodium: 870mg
- Fiber: 3g

Yogurt Parfait with Granola

Difficulty Level: ★☆☆☆☆

Total Time: 10 minutes

Servings: 2

Ingredients:

- 1 cup Greek yogurt
- 1/2 cup granola
- 1/2 cup mixed berries (strawberries, blueberries, raspberries)
- 2 tablespoons honey or maple syrup
- Optional toppings: sliced almonds, coconut flakes, chia seeds

Required Equipment:

- 2 glasses or mason jars
- Spoon

Preparation:

1. Start by placing 1/4 cup of Greek yogurt at the bottom of each glass or mason jar.
2. Add a layer of 1/4 cup granola over the yogurt in each glass.

3. Place a layer of mixed berries on top of the granola.

4. Drizzle 1 tablespoon of honey or maple syrup over the berries in each glass.

5. Repeat the layering process by adding another 1/4 cup of Greek yogurt on top of the berries in each glass.

6. Finish off with a final layer of granola and a few more berries on top for garnish. If desired, add optional toppings like sliced almonds, coconut flakes, or chia seeds for extra texture and flavor.

7. Serve immediately or cover and refrigerate for up to 1 hour before serving.

Chef's Tip:

- For a personalized touch, feel free to swap out the mixed berries with any fruit of your choice. Mango, peach slices, or kiwi make great alternatives.
- If you prefer your granola with a bit more crunch, add it just before serving to prevent it from getting too soft in the yogurt.

Nutritional Information per Serving:

- Calories: 280
- Protein: 12g
- Carbohydrates: 44g
- Fat: 7g
- Sugar: 24g
- Fiber: 4g

Cinnamon French Toast

Difficulty Level: ★☆☆☆☆

Total Time: 30 minutes

Servings: 4

Ingredients:
- 8 slices of thick-cut bread (brioche or challah works best)
- 4 large eggs
- 1 cup whole milk
- 1/4 cup granulated sugar
- 1 tsp vanilla extract
- 1 tsp ground cinnamon
- 1/4 tsp ground nutmeg
- Butter, for frying

- Maple syrup, for serving
- Powdered sugar, for dusting (optional)
- Fresh berries, for garnish (optional)

Required Equipment:
- Large mixing bowl
- Whisk
- Non-stick skillet or griddle
- Spatula
- Measuring cups and spoons

Preparation:

1. In a large mixing bowl, whisk together eggs, milk, granulated sugar, vanilla extract, ground cinnamon, and ground nutmeg until well combined.
2. Preheat your skillet or griddle over medium heat and add a small amount of butter to coat the surface.
3. Dip each slice of bread into the egg mixture, allowing it to soak for a few seconds on each side. Make sure the bread is fully coated but not soggy.
4. Place the soaked bread slices onto the heated skillet. Cook for 2-3 minutes on each side or until each side is golden brown and crispy.
5. Repeat with the remaining slices of bread, adding more butter to the skillet as needed.
6. Serve the French toast warm, topped with maple syrup, a dusting of powdered sugar, and fresh berries if desired.

Chef's Tip:
- For an extra rich flavor, try using half-and-half instead of whole milk.
- If you prefer your French toast with a bit more spice, feel free to increase the amount of cinnamon or nutmeg according to your taste.
- Leftover French toast can be stored in the refrigerator and reheated in a toaster or oven for a quick breakfast.

Nutritional Information per Serving:
- Calories: 320
- Fat: 14g
- Carbohydrates: 40g
- Protein: 12g
- Sugar: 22g
- Sodium: 410mg

Veggie Breakfast Scramble

Difficulty Level: ★☆☆☆☆

Total Time: 25 minutes

Servings: 2

Ingredients:
- 4 large eggs
- 1/4 cup milk
- 1/2 cup diced bell peppers (mix of colors)
- 1/4 cup diced onions
- 1/2 cup chopped spinach
- 1/4 cup shredded cheddar cheese
- Salt and pepper to taste
- 1 tablespoon olive oil

Required Equipment:
- Non-stick skillet
- Mixing bowl
- Whisk
- Spatula

Preparation:

1. In a mixing bowl, whisk together the eggs, milk, salt, and pepper until well combined and slightly frothy.
2. Heat the olive oil in a non-stick skillet over medium heat.
3. Add the diced onions and bell peppers to the skillet. Sauté for 3-4 minutes until the vegetables are soft.
4. Stir in the chopped spinach and cook for an additional 1-2 minutes, until the spinach has wilted.
5. Pour the egg mixture over the sautéed vegetables in the skillet. Let it sit without stirring for about 20 seconds, then gently stir with a spatula, pushing the cooked edges towards the center.
6. Sprinkle the shredded cheddar cheese evenly over the top of the eggs. Cover the skillet with a lid and reduce the heat to low. Cook for 2-3 minutes, or until the cheese is melted and the eggs are set to your liking.
7. Divide the scramble between two plates and serve immediately.

Chef's Tip:
- For a spicier scramble, add a pinch of red pepper flakes to the egg mixture before cooking.
- Feel free to swap out or add any vegetables you have on hand. Mushrooms, tomatoes, and zucchini make great additions.

- To make this dish even more filling, serve it with a side of whole-grain toast or wrap it in a tortilla for a breakfast burrito.

Nutritional Information per Serving:

- Calories: 280
- Protein: 18g
- Carbohydrates: 8g
- Fat: 20g
- Sodium: 340mg
- Fiber: 2g

Peanut Butter and Banana Oatmeal

Difficulty Level: ★☆☆☆☆

Total Time: 15 minutes

Servings: 2

Ingredients:

- 1 cup rolled oats
- 2 cups water or milk (for creamier oatmeal, use milk)
- 1/4 teaspoon salt
- 2 tablespoons peanut butter
- 1 ripe banana, sliced
- 2 teaspoons honey or maple syrup (optional)
- A sprinkle of cinnamon (optional)
- A handful of chopped nuts (optional, for topping)

Required Equipment:

- Medium saucepan
- Measuring cups and spoons
- Knife
- Spoon for stirring

Preparation:

1. In a medium saucepan, bring 2 cups of water or milk to a boil. Add a 1/4 teaspoon of salt to the liquid.

2. Stir in 1 cup of rolled oats and reduce the heat to medium. Cook for 5 minutes, stirring occasionally, until the oats are soft and have absorbed most of the liquid.

3. Remove the saucepan from the heat and let it sit covered for 2 minutes. The oatmeal will thicken further as it cools.

4. Stir in 2 tablespoons of peanut butter into the oatmeal until well combined.

5. Divide the oatmeal into two bowls. Top each bowl with half of the sliced banana.

6. Drizzle each serving with 1 teaspoon of honey or maple syrup if desired. Add a sprinkle of cinnamon and a handful of chopped nuts for extra flavor and crunch.

Chef's Tip:

- For a vegan version, use water or a plant-based milk and maple syrup as the sweetener.
- Feel free to add more toppings like fresh berries, chia seeds, or a dollop of Greek yogurt to make your oatmeal even more nutritious and filling.
- If you prefer your oatmeal a bit thinner, add a splash more milk or water until you reach your desired consistency.

Nutritional Information per Serving:

- Calories: 280 (varies depending on milk choice and toppings)
- Protein: 9g
- Carbohydrates: 45g
- Fat: 8g
- Fiber: 6g
- Sugar: 10g (varies with sweetener and banana size)

Spinach and Feta Breakfast Wrap

Difficulty Level: ★★☆☆☆ (Easy)

Ingredients:

- 2 large eggs
- 1/2 cup fresh spinach, chopped
- 2 tablespoons feta cheese, crumbled
- 1 whole wheat tortilla
- 1 teaspoon olive oil

- Salt and pepper to taste

Instructions:

1. Heat olive oil in a non-stick pan over medium heat.
2. Add spinach and sauté until wilted.
3. Whisk eggs, season with salt and pepper, and pour into the pan.
4. Stir gently until eggs are scrambled and cooked.
5. Place the eggs and spinach mixture onto the tortilla, sprinkle with feta cheese, and wrap tightly.

Nutritional Information (per serving):

- Calories: 280
- Protein: 16g
- Carbohydrates: 21g
- Fat: 15g

Apple Cinnamon Overnight Oats

Difficulty Level: ★☆☆☆☆ (Very Easy)

Ingredients:

- 1/2 cup rolled oats
- 1/2 cup milk (or plant-based alternative)
- 1/4 cup Greek yogurt
- 1/4 teaspoon cinnamon
- 1/2 apple, diced
- 1 teaspoon honey (optional)

Instructions:

1. In a mason jar or small bowl, combine oats, milk, yogurt, and cinnamon.
2. Stir well, then layer with diced apple.
3. Drizzle honey on top if desired.
4. Cover and refrigerate overnight. Enjoy cold or warmed up the next morning.

Nutritional Information (per serving):

- Calories: 210
- Protein: 8g
- Carbohydrates: 35g

- Fat: 4g

Cheesy Veggie Egg Muffins

Difficulty Level: ★★☆☆☆ (Easy)

Ingredients:

- 4 large eggs
- 1/2 cup shredded cheddar cheese
- 1/2 cup diced bell peppers
- 1/4 cup chopped green onions
- Salt and pepper to taste
- Non-stick cooking spray

Instructions:

1. Preheat oven to 375°F (190°C). Grease a muffin tin with cooking spray.
2. In a bowl, whisk eggs and season with salt and pepper.
3. Mix in cheese, bell peppers, and green onions.
4. Pour mixture evenly into muffin cups.
5. Bake for 15-18 minutes or until eggs are set.

Nutritional Information (per muffin):

- Calories: 90
- Protein: 7g
- Carbohydrates: 1g
- Fat: 6g

Sweet Potato Breakfast Hash

Difficulty Level: ★★★☆☆ (Moderate)

Ingredients:

- 1 medium sweet potato, peeled and diced
- 1/4 cup diced onion
- 1/4 cup diced bell pepper
- 2 tablespoons olive oil

- 2 large eggs
- Salt and pepper to taste

Instructions:

1. Heat olive oil in a large skillet over medium heat.
2. Add sweet potatoes and cook for 10 minutes, stirring occasionally.
3. Add onion and bell pepper, cooking until soft.
4. Create two small wells in the hash, crack an egg into each, and cover the skillet.
5. Cook until eggs reach desired doneness.

Nutritional Information (per serving):

- Calories: 350
- Protein: 12g
- Carbohydrates: 28g
- Fat: 22g

Strawberry Banana Breakfast Quesadilla

Difficulty Level: ★★☆☆☆ (Easy)

Ingredients:

- 1 whole wheat tortilla
- 2 tablespoons cream cheese
- 1/4 cup sliced strawberries
- 1/4 cup sliced banana
- 1 teaspoon honey
- Non-stick cooking spray

Instructions:
1. Spread cream cheese evenly over half of the tortilla.
2. Layer with strawberries and banana slices, then drizzle with honey.
3. Fold the tortilla in half.
4. Heat a skillet over medium heat and spray with non-stick cooking spray.
5. Cook the quesadilla for 2-3 minutes on each side until golden brown.

Nutritional Information (per serving):
- Calories: 290
- Protein: 8g
- Carbohydrates: 38g
- Fat: 10g

Chapter 3: 10 Easy Snack Recipes

Trail Mix Energy Bites

Difficulty Level: ★☆☆☆☆

Total Time: 15 minutes

Servings: 12 bites

Ingredients:
- 1 cup rolled oats
- 1/2 cup peanut butter
- 1/3 cup honey
- 1/2 cup mini chocolate chips
- 1/2 cup dried cranberries
- 1/4 cup sunflower seeds
- 1 teaspoon vanilla extract

Required Equipment:
- Large mixing bowl
- Measuring cups and spoons
- Spatula
- Baking sheet
- Parchment paper

Preparation:

1. In a large mixing bowl, combine 1 cup rolled oats, 1/2 cup peanut butter, 1/3 cup honey, and 1 teaspoon vanilla extract. Mix well with a spatula until the ingredients are thoroughly blended.

2. Add 1/2 cup mini chocolate chips, 1/2 cup dried cranberries, and 1/4 cup sunflower seeds to the bowl. Stir the mixture until the add-ins are evenly distributed throughout.

3. Lay a piece of parchment paper on a baking sheet. Using your hands, roll the mixture into 12 evenly sized balls, each about the size of a golf ball, and place them on the parchment paper.

4. Chill the energy bites in the refrigerator for at least 1 hour to set. This makes them easier to handle and keeps them firm.

5. Once chilled, the trail mix energy bites are ready to be enjoyed. Store any leftovers in an airtight container in the refrigerator.

Chef's Tip:

- Feel free to customize your energy bites by adding other ingredients such as chopped nuts, flaxseeds, or coconut flakes for extra flavor and nutrition.

- If the mixture is too sticky to handle, wet your hands slightly before rolling the balls to prevent sticking.

- For a nut-free version, substitute sunflower seed butter or tahini for the peanut butter.

Nutritional Information per Serving:

- Calories: 180

- Protein: 4g

- Fat: 9g

- Carbohydrates: 24g

- Fiber: 2g

- Sugar: 16g

Cheesy Garlic Breadsticks

Difficulty Level: ★☆☆☆☆

Total Time: 20 minutes

Servings: 4

Ingredients:

- 1 pound of pizza dough (store-bought or homemade)

- 2 tablespoons olive oil

- 2 cloves garlic, minced

- 1 cup shredded mozzarella cheese

- 1/4 cup grated Parmesan cheese

- 1 teaspoon dried Italian seasoning

- 1/2 teaspoon garlic powder

- 1/4 teaspoon salt

- Marinara sauce, for dipping

Required Equipment:

- Baking sheet

- Parchment paper

- Small bowl

- Brush (for oil)

- Cheese grater (if needed)

- Knife or pizza cutter

Preparation:

1. Preheat your oven to 425°F (220°C). Line a baking sheet with parchment paper to prevent sticking.

2. Roll out the pizza dough on a lightly floured surface to about 1/2 inch thickness. Transfer the dough to the prepared baking sheet.

3. In a small bowl, mix together the olive oil and minced garlic. Brush this mixture evenly over the top of the dough.

4. Sprinkle the shredded mozzarella cheese, grated Parmesan cheese, dried Italian seasoning, garlic powder, and salt evenly over the garlic oil-brushed dough.

5. Bake in the preheated oven for 12-15 minutes, or until the cheese is bubbly and golden and the edges of the dough are crisp.

6. Remove from the oven and let cool for a couple of minutes. Then, using a knife or pizza cutter, slice the bread into sticks.

7. Serve warm with marinara sauce on the side for dipping.

Chef's Tip:

- For an extra crispy bottom, you can preheat your baking sheet in the oven as it warms up. Just be careful when transferring the dough to the hot baking sheet.

- Feel free to customize your breadsticks by adding toppings like sliced olives, diced bell peppers, or even a sprinkle of chili flakes for a spicy kick.

- If using store-bought pizza dough, let it sit at room temperature for about 20 minutes before rolling it out. This makes it easier to handle and shape.

Nutritional Information per Serving:

- Calories: 300
- Protein: 12g
- Fat: 15g
- Carbohydrates: 30g
- Fiber: 1g
- Sugar: 4g

Mini Caprese Skewers

Difficulty Level: ★☆☆☆☆

Total Time: 15 minutes

Servings: 4

Ingredients:

- 16 cherry tomatoes

- 16 small balls of fresh mozzarella cheese (bocconcini)

- 16 fresh basil leaves

- 2 tablespoons extra-virgin olive oil

- 1 tablespoon balsamic glaze

- Salt and pepper to taste

- 16 toothpicks

Required Equipment:

- Toothpicks

- Small bowl

- Spoon

Preparation:

1. Wash the cherry tomatoes and basil leaves gently under cold water. Pat them dry with a paper towel.

2. Take a toothpick and skewer one cherry tomato, one basil leaf (folded if large), and one ball of mozzarella cheese, in that order.

3. Repeat the process with the remaining tomatoes, basil leaves, and mozzarella balls until you have 16 mini skewers.

4. Arrange the mini skewers on a serving platter.

5. In a small bowl, whisk together the extra-virgin olive oil and balsamic glaze. Drizzle this mixture over the skewers.

6. Season the mini caprese skewers with salt and pepper to taste.

7. Serve immediately or cover and refrigerate until ready to serve.

Chef's Tip:

- For a fun variation, try using different colored cherry tomatoes to make the platter more vibrant.

- If balsamic glaze is too strong for your taste, you can dilute it with a bit more olive oil or use a light drizzle of honey instead.

- These skewers can be made a few hours ahead of time. Just be sure to add the dressing right before serving to keep everything fresh.

Nutritional Information per Serving:

- Calories: 150

- Protein: 8g

- Fat: 12g

- Carbohydrates: 4g

- Sugar: 2g

- Sodium: 200mg

Spicy Popcorn

Difficulty Level: ★☆☆☆☆

Total Time: 15 minutes

Servings: 4

Ingredients:
- 1/2 cup unpopped popcorn kernels
- 2 tablespoons coconut oil (or vegetable oil)
- 1 teaspoon smoked paprika
- 1/2 teaspoon garlic powder
- 1/4 teaspoon cayenne pepper (adjust to taste)
- 1/2 teaspoon salt

Required Equipment:
- Large pot with lid
- Measuring spoons
- Large bowl

Preparation:

1. Heat the coconut oil in a large pot over medium heat. Test the heat by adding a single popcorn kernel to the pot. When the kernel pops, the oil is ready.

2. Add the rest of the popcorn kernels to the pot and cover with the lid. Gently shake the pot back and forth over the burner.

3. Listen for the popping sounds. Once the popping slows to about 2 seconds between pops, remove the pot from heat. Keep the lid on until the popping stops completely to avoid any unpopped kernels from escaping.

4. In a small bowl, mix together the smoked paprika, garlic powder, cayenne pepper, and salt.

5. Transfer the popped popcorn to a large bowl. While the popcorn is still warm, sprinkle the spice mix over it. Toss well to ensure the popcorn is evenly coated with the spices.

Chef's Tip:
- For an extra kick, add a pinch of chili powder or increase the amount of cayenne pepper.
- If you prefer a buttery flavor, melt 2 tablespoons of unsalted butter and drizzle it over the popcorn before adding the spice mix.

- To ensure even coating, you can also put the popcorn and spice mix in a large paper bag, close the top, and shake vigorously.

Nutritional Information per Serving:

- Calories: 150

- Fat: 9g

- Sodium: 290mg

- Carbohydrates: 16g

- Fiber: 3g

- Protein: 2g

Veggie Spring Rolls

Difficulty Level: ★★☆☆☆

Total Time: 30 minutes

Servings: 4

Ingredients:
- 8 rice paper wrappers
- 1 cup vermicelli noodles, cooked and cooled
- 1 cup thinly sliced cabbage
- 1 carrot, julienned
- 1 cucumber, julienned
- 1 bell pepper, thinly sliced
- 1/4 cup fresh mint leaves
- 1/4 cup fresh cilantro leaves
- Peanut sauce, for dipping

Required Equipment:
- Large bowl of warm water
- Clean, damp kitchen towel
- Cutting board
- Knife

Preparation:

1. Fill a large bowl with warm water. Dip one rice paper wrapper into the water for about 15-20 seconds until it is just soft. Lay the wrapper flat on a clean, damp kitchen towel.

2. On the lower third of the wrapper, place a small handful of vermicelli noodles.

3. Add a few slices of cabbage, carrot, cucumber, and bell pepper on top of the noodles.

4. Sprinkle a few mint and cilantro leaves over the vegetables.

5. Carefully fold the bottom edge of the wrapper over the filling. Then, fold in the sides and continue rolling tightly until the spring roll is completely sealed. Repeat with the remaining wrappers and filling.

6. Serve the veggie spring rolls with peanut sauce for dipping.

Chef's Tip:

- Keep the rice paper wrappers covered with a damp cloth after soaking to prevent them from drying out before you roll them.

- Feel free to experiment with the fillings based on your preferences or what you have available. Avocado, shrimp, or tofu are great additions.

- If the rice paper tears while you're rolling, simply wet another wrapper and wrap it around the first one for extra support.

Nutritional Information per Serving:

- Calories: 150
- Protein: 3g
- Fat: 1g
- Carbohydrates: 34g
- Fiber: 2g
- Sugar: 3g

Sweet Potato Fries

Difficulty Level: ★☆☆☆☆

Total Time: 35 minutes

Servings: 4

Ingredients:

- 2 large sweet potatoes, peeled and cut into 1/4 inch thick sticks
- 2 tablespoons olive oil
- 1/2 teaspoon paprika
- 1/2 teaspoon garlic powder
- Salt and pepper to taste
- Optional: 1/4 teaspoon cayenne pepper for a spicy kick

Required Equipment:

- Baking sheet
- Parchment paper
- Large bowl
- Measuring spoons

Preparation:

1. Preheat your oven to 425°F (220°C). Line a baking sheet with parchment paper to prevent the sweet potato fries from sticking.

2. In a large bowl, toss the sweet potato sticks with olive oil, paprika, garlic powder, salt, and pepper until they are evenly coated. If you like your fries with a bit of heat, add the optional cayenne pepper.

3. Spread the sweet potato fries in a single layer on the prepared baking sheet. Make sure they are not touching each other too much to ensure they get crispy.

4. Bake in the preheated oven for 25-30 minutes, flipping the fries halfway through the cooking time, until they are golden brown and crispy on the edges.

5. Remove the sweet potato fries from the oven and let them cool for a few minutes on the baking sheet before serving. This allows them to crisp up even more.

Chef's Tip:

- For extra flavor, try sprinkling your finished sweet potato fries with a little grated Parmesan cheese or fresh chopped herbs like parsley or cilantro.

- Sweet potato fries are best enjoyed fresh, but if you have leftovers, reheat them in the oven at 425°F (220°C) for 5-10 minutes to get them crispy again.

Nutritional Information per Serving:

- Calories: 200
- Fat: 7g
- Saturated Fat: 1g
- Sodium: 120mg
- Carbohydrates: 34g
- Fiber: 5g
- Sugar: 7g
- Protein: 2g

Hummus and Veggie Cups

Difficulty Level: ★☆☆☆

Total Time: 15 minutes

Servings: 4

Ingredients:
- 1 cup store-bought or homemade hummus
- 1 large carrot, peeled and cut into sticks
- 1 cucumber, sliced into sticks
- 1 bell pepper (any color), sliced into sticks
- 1/2 cup cherry tomatoes, halved
- 4 small whole wheat pita breads, quartered
- 4 small clear cups or glasses

Required Equipment:
- Knife
- Cutting board
- 4 small clear cups or glasses

Preparation:

1. Begin by preparing your vegetables. Wash and dry the carrot, cucumber, bell pepper, and cherry tomatoes. Peel the carrot. Using a knife and cutting board, cut the carrot and cucumber into sticks approximately 3 inches long. Slice the bell pepper into similar-sized sticks and halve the cherry tomatoes.

2. Take the whole wheat pita breads and quarter them. Each pita bread should be cut into 4 equal pieces, making them easy to dip.

3. Spoon a generous amount of hummus into each clear cup or glass, filling about a quarter of the cup.

4. Arrange the vegetable sticks and pita bread quarters vertically in the cups, sticking them into the hummus so they stand upright. Distribute the colors and types of vegetables evenly among the cups for a visually appealing presentation.

5. Place the cherry tomato halves on top of the hummus around the base of the vegetable sticks to add a pop of color and additional flavor.

Chef's Tip:
- For a fun twist, try using different flavored hummus varieties like roasted red pepper or garlic to mix things up.
- These veggie cups can be customized with any of your favorite vegetables. Try adding celery sticks, radishes, or even broccoli florets for more variety.
- If you're preparing these cups for a gathering, consider wrapping them with a small piece of plastic wrap for easy transport and freshness.

Nutritional Information per Serving:

- Calories: 180
- Protein: 6g
- Fat: 8g
- Carbohydrates: 24g
- Fiber: 5g
- Sugar: 4g

Apple Nachos

Difficulty Level: ★☆☆☆

Total Time: 10 minutes

Servings: 2-4

Ingredients:
- 2 large apples (any variety, but Granny Smith or Fuji work well for a mix of tart and sweet)
- 1/4 cup creamy peanut butter, melted
- 1/4 cup chocolate chips, melted
- 1/4 cup granola
- 2 tablespoons dried cranberries or raisins
- Optional toppings: chopped nuts, mini marshmallows, coconut flakes

Required Equipment:
- Knife
- Cutting board
- Microwave-safe bowls (2)
- Spoon

Preparation:

1. Wash the apples thoroughly and pat them dry with a paper towel. Core the apples and slice them into thin rounds, about 1/4 inch thick. Arrange the apple slices on a large plate or platter, slightly overlapping.

2. In a microwave-safe bowl, melt the peanut butter on high for about 30 seconds or until it's runny. Use a spoon to drizzle the melted peanut butter evenly over the apple slices.

3. In another microwave-safe bowl, melt the chocolate chips in 30-second intervals, stirring in between, until smooth and fully melted. Drizzle the melted chocolate over the apple slices, on top of the peanut butter.

4. Sprinkle the granola and dried cranberries (or raisins) over the apples. Add any additional optional toppings you like.

5. Serve immediately, or if you prefer the toppings to set a bit, chill in the refrigerator for about 5 minutes before serving.

Chef's Tip:

- For an extra fun twist, use cookie cutters to cut the apple slices into shapes before adding the toppings.
- If you're allergic to peanut butter, almond butter or sunflower seed butter make great alternatives.
- To prevent the apple slices from browning, you can lightly brush them with lemon juice before adding the toppings.

Nutritional Information per Serving:

- Calories: Approximately 200 (varies with toppings)
- Protein: 4g
- Fat: 10g
- Carbohydrates: 28g
- Fiber: 4g
- Sugar: 20g

Zucchini Chips

Difficulty Level: ★☆☆☆☆

Total Time: 40 minutes

Servings: 4

Ingredients:

- 2 medium zucchinis
- 1 tablespoon olive oil
- 1/4 teaspoon salt
- 1/4 teaspoon garlic powder
- 1/4 teaspoon paprika (optional)

Required Equipment:

- Cutting board
- Sharp knife
- Mixing bowl
- Baking sheet

- Parchment paper

Preparation:

1. Preheat your oven to 225°F (107°C). Line a baking sheet with parchment paper.

2. Wash the zucchinis and slice them into thin rounds, about 1/8 inch thick, using a sharp knife on a cutting board.

3. In a mixing bowl, toss the zucchini slices with olive oil, salt, garlic powder, and paprika (if using) until evenly coated.

4. Arrange the zucchini slices in a single layer on the prepared baking sheet, making sure they do not overlap.

5. Bake in the preheated oven for 30-35 minutes, then flip each slice and bake for an additional 30-35 minutes, or until the chips are crispy and lightly browned.

6. Remove the baking sheet from the oven and allow the zucchini chips to cool on the baking sheet for 10 minutes; they will continue to crisp up as they cool.

Chef's Tip:
- For extra flavor, try adding a sprinkle of grated Parmesan cheese or nutritional yeast over the zucchini slices before baking.
- Keep an eye on the chips during the last few minutes of baking to prevent them from burning, as oven temperatures can vary.
- These zucchini chips are best enjoyed the day they are made but can be stored in an airtight container for up to 24 hours.

Nutritional Information per Serving:
- Calories: 60
- Protein: 1g
- Fat: 5g
- Carbohydrates: 4g
- Fiber: 1g
- Sugar: 2g

Chocolate-Dipped Pretzels

Difficulty Level: ★☆☆☆☆

Total Time: 20 minutes

Servings: 4

Ingredients:

- 1 bag (16 oz) of pretzel rods or twists
- 2 cups (12 oz) semi-sweet chocolate chips
- 1 tablespoon vegetable oil
- Assorted sprinkles or crushed nuts for decoration

Required Equipment:

- Microwave-safe bowl
- Baking sheet
- Parchment paper
- Spatula or spoon
- Small bowls for sprinkles and nuts

Preparation:

1. Line a baking sheet with parchment paper and set aside.

2. In a microwave-safe bowl, combine the chocolate chips and vegetable oil. Microwave on high for 30 seconds, then stir. Continue to microwave in 15-second intervals, stirring after each, until the chocolate is fully melted and smooth.

3. Dip each pretzel rod into the melted chocolate, using a spoon or spatula to help spread the chocolate evenly. Shake off any excess chocolate.

4. Before the chocolate sets, sprinkle your choice of decorations over the chocolate-covered section of the pretzels. You can use assorted sprinkles, crushed nuts, or even mini chocolate chips for extra fun.

5. Lay the decorated pretzels on the prepared baking sheet. Allow them to sit at room temperature until the chocolate hardens, about 15 minutes. For quicker setting, you can place the baking sheet in the refrigerator for about 10 minutes.

6. Once the chocolate is set, the pretzels are ready to serve. Enjoy as a snack or package them up for a sweet gift.

Chef's Tip:

- For a fun variation, try using white chocolate or dark chocolate instead of semi-sweet. You can even drizzle a second type of melted chocolate over the first for a fancy, two-tone effect.

- If you're feeling adventurous, try adding a small amount of flavored extract (like peppermint or orange) to the melted chocolate for a flavor twist.

- To make dipping easier, if using pretzel rods, tilt the bowl so the chocolate pools to one side, allowing for more coverage as you dip.

Nutritional Information per Serving:

- Calories: 220 (varies depending on toppings)
- Protein: 3g
- Fat: 12g
- Carbohydrates: 28g
- Fiber: 2g
- Sugar: 16g

Peanut Butter Apple Sandwiches

Difficulty Level: ★☆☆☆☆ (Very Easy)

Ingredients:

- 1 large apple (sliced into rings)
- 2 tablespoons peanut butter
- 2 tablespoons granola
- 1 teaspoon honey (optional)

Instructions:

1. Spread peanut butter on one side of each apple slice.
2. Sprinkle granola evenly on top.
3. Drizzle with honey if desired.
4. Place another apple slice on top to form a sandwich.

Nutritional Information (per sandwich):

- Calories: 140
- Protein: 4g
- Carbohydrates: 20g
- Fat: 6g

Cucumber and Cream Cheese Roll-Ups

Difficulty Level: ★★☆☆☆ (Easy)

Ingredients:

- 1 large cucumber
- 4 tablespoons cream cheese
- 2 tablespoons finely chopped dill or chives
- 4 slices of turkey or ham (optional)

Instructions:

1. Use a vegetable peeler to slice the cucumber into thin strips.
2. Spread cream cheese onto each strip and sprinkle with dill or chives.
3. Place a slice of turkey or ham on top (optional).
4. Roll the strips tightly and secure with a toothpick.

Nutritional Information (per roll-up):

- Calories: 35
- Protein: 2g
- Carbohydrates: 2g
- Fat: 2g

Baked Parmesan Kale Chips

Difficulty Level: ★★☆☆☆ (Easy)

Ingredients:

- 1 bunch of kale
- 2 tablespoons olive oil
- 2 tablespoons grated Parmesan cheese
- Salt and pepper to taste

Instructions:

1. Preheat the oven to 350°F (175°C).
2. Wash and dry kale thoroughly, then tear into bite-sized pieces.
3. Toss the kale with olive oil, Parmesan, salt, and pepper.
4. Spread the kale evenly on a baking sheet.
5. Bake for 10-15 minutes, or until crispy.

Nutritional Information (per serving):

- Calories: 90
- Protein: 3g
- Carbohydrates: 4g
- Fat: 7g

Greek Yogurt Fruit Dip with Strawberries

Difficulty Level: ★☆☆☆☆ (Very Easy)

Ingredients:

- 1/2 cup plain Greek yogurt
- 1 tablespoon honey
- 1/4 teaspoon vanilla extract
- 1 cup fresh strawberries

Instructions:

1. In a small bowl, mix the Greek yogurt, honey, and vanilla extract until smooth.
2. Serve the dip with fresh strawberries on the side.

Nutritional Information (per serving):

- Calories: 80
- Protein: 5g
- Carbohydrates: 12g
- Fat: 1g

Avocado Toast Bites

Difficulty Level: ★★☆☆☆ (Easy)

Ingredients:

- 4 slices whole-grain bread (cut into quarters)
- 1 ripe avocado
- 1/2 teaspoon lemon juice
- Salt, pepper, and chili flakes to taste

Instructions:

1. Toast the bread slices until golden.
2. Mash the avocado in a bowl with lemon juice, salt, and pepper.
3. Spread the avocado mixture onto each toast quarter.
4. Sprinkle with chili flakes for added flavor.

Nutritional Information (per bite):

- Calories: 60
- Protein: 1g
- Carbohydrates: 6g
- Fat: 3g

Chapter 4: 10 Lunch Recipes

Grilled Cheese Sandwich

Difficulty Level: ★☆☆☆☆

Total Time: 10 minutes

Servings: 1

Ingredients:
- 2 slices of bread (white or whole wheat)
- 2 slices of cheddar cheese
- 1 tablespoon unsalted butter

Required Equipment:
- Skillet or frying pan
- Spatula
- Knife (for spreading butter)

Preparation:

1. Heat the skillet over medium heat.
2. Spread butter evenly on one side of each bread slice. Place one slice, butter-side down, in the skillet.
3. Lay the cheddar cheese slices on top of the bread in the skillet, then cover with the second slice of bread, butter-side up.
4. Cook for about 2-3 minutes, or until the bottom slice is golden brown. Use the spatula to carefully flip the sandwich.
5. Cook for another 2-3 minutes, pressing down lightly with the spatula to ensure even cooking, until the second side is golden brown and the cheese is melted.
6. Remove the sandwich from the skillet and let it cool for a minute before cutting into halves or quarters.

Chef's Tip:
- For a gourmet twist, add a slice of tomato, some cooked bacon, or a few leaves of spinach inside the sandwich before cooking.
- If you prefer a crunchier texture, try using a hearty sourdough or multigrain bread.
- To avoid burning the sandwich, keep an eye on the heat and adjust it as necessary. If the skillet gets too hot, the bread may burn before the cheese has a chance to melt.

Nutritional Information per Serving:

- Calories: 400

- Protein: 15g

- Carbohydrates: 30g

- Fat: 25g

- Sodium: 720mg

- Fiber: 2g

Turkey and Avocado Wrap

Difficulty Level: ★☆☆☆☆

Total Time: 10 minutes

Servings: 2

Ingredients:

- 2 large flour tortillas

- 1/2 pound sliced turkey breast

- 1 ripe avocado, sliced

- 1/4 cup shredded lettuce

- 1/4 cup diced tomatoes

- 1/4 cup shredded cheddar cheese

- 2 tablespoons ranch dressing

- Salt and pepper to taste

Required Equipment:

- Knife

- Cutting board

- Spoon

Preparation:

1. Lay the flour tortillas flat on a clean surface.

2. Evenly distribute the sliced turkey breast over the center of each tortilla.

3. Place the sliced avocado on top of the turkey slices.

4. Sprinkle the shredded lettuce and diced tomatoes over the avocado.

5. Add the shredded cheddar cheese on top of the vegetables.

6. Drizzle each tortilla with 1 tablespoon of ranch dressing. Season with salt and pepper to taste.

7. Carefully fold the bottom edge of each tortilla up over the fillings. Then, fold in the sides and roll tightly to enclose all the ingredients.

8. Cut each wrap in half diagonally with a knife.

Chef's Tip:

- For a healthier version, use whole wheat or spinach tortillas instead of flour tortillas.

- Feel free to add or substitute ingredients based on your preferences. Cucumbers, bell peppers, or onions make great additions.

- If you prefer a warm wrap, heat the tortillas in a microwave for 10-15 seconds before assembling.

Nutritional Information per Serving:

- Calories: 350

- Protein: 25g

- Carbohydrates: 27g

- Fat: 17g

- Fiber: 5g

- Sugar: 3g

Chicken Caesar Salad

Difficulty Level: ★★☆☆☆

Total Time: 20 minutes

Servings: 4

Ingredients:

- 2 boneless, skinless chicken breasts

- 1 teaspoon olive oil

- Salt and pepper, to taste

- 4 cups chopped romaine lettuce

- 1/2 cup croutons

- 1/4 cup grated Parmesan cheese

- 1/2 cup Caesar dressing

Required Equipment:

- Grill pan or skillet

- Meat thermometer

- Cutting board

- Knife

- Large mixing bowl
- Tongs

Preparation:

1. Preheat your grill pan or skillet over medium-high heat and brush it with olive oil.

2. Season both sides of the chicken breasts with salt and pepper. Place the chicken in the pan and cook for about 6-7 minutes on each side, or until the internal temperature reaches 165°F (74°C). Use a meat thermometer to ensure it's cooked through.

3. Transfer the cooked chicken to a cutting board and let it rest for a few minutes. Then, slice it into thin strips.

4. In a large mixing bowl, combine the chopped romaine lettuce, croutons, and grated Parmesan cheese.

5. Add the Caesar dressing to the salad and toss well to coat all the ingredients evenly.

6. Divide the salad among four plates. Top each serving with an equal amount of sliced chicken.

7. Serve immediately.

Chef's Tip:

- For a lighter version, you can substitute the Caesar dressing with a homemade dressing made from Greek yogurt, lemon juice, minced garlic, and a touch of Dijon mustard.

- To add an extra crunch, try making your own croutons by cubing whole-grain bread, tossing it with olive oil and your favorite seasonings, and baking until crispy.

- If you're short on time, using pre-cooked chicken or rotisserie chicken from the grocery store is a great shortcut. Just slice or shred it before adding to your salad.

Nutritional Information per Serving:

- Calories: 320
- Protein: 28g
- Fat: 18g
- Carbohydrates: 12g
- Fiber: 2g
- Sugar: 3g

Veggie Quesadilla

Difficulty Level: ★☆☆☆☆

Total Time: 20 minutes

Servings: 4

Ingredients:

- 4 large flour tortillas
- 1 cup shredded cheddar cheese
- 1 cup shredded Monterey Jack cheese
- 1 cup black beans, rinsed and drained
- 1 cup corn kernels (fresh, canned, or thawed from frozen)
- 1/2 cup diced red bell pepper
- 1/2 cup diced green bell pepper
- 1/4 cup finely chopped red onion
- 1/4 cup chopped fresh cilantro
- 1 teaspoon ground cumin
- Salt and pepper to taste
- Olive oil or cooking spray

Required Equipment:

- Large skillet or griddle
- Cheese grater (if cheese is not pre-shredded)
- Knife
- Cutting board
- Spatula

Preparation:

1. Heat a large skillet or griddle over medium heat. Lightly brush one side of each tortilla with olive oil or spray with cooking spray.

2. Place one tortilla, oil side down, on the skillet. On half of the tortilla, sprinkle a quarter of the cheddar and Monterey Jack cheeses, followed by a quarter of the black beans, corn, red and green bell peppers, red onion, and cilantro. Sprinkle with a little ground cumin, salt, and pepper.

3. Fold the other half of the tortilla over the filled half to form a half-moon shape. Press down lightly with a spatula to ensure the quesadilla sticks together.

4. Cook for 2-3 minutes, or until the bottom of the tortilla is golden brown and crispy. Carefully flip the quesadilla with a spatula and cook for another 2-3 minutes on the other side, ensuring the cheese is melted and the tortilla is crispy.

5. Remove the quesadilla from the skillet and place it on a cutting board. Let it cool for 1 minute before cutting into wedges. Repeat the process with the remaining tortillas and filling ingredients.

6. Serve the quesadilla wedges warm, with salsa, sour cream, or guacamole on the side if desired.

Chef's Tip:

- For a protein boost, add cooked shredded chicken, beef, or pork to the filling.
- Customize your quesadilla with other vegetables like spinach, mushrooms, or zucchini for added nutrition and flavor.
- To keep quesadillas warm while cooking in batches, place them on a baking sheet in a preheated 200°F oven.

Nutritional Information per Serving:

- Calories: 350
- Protein: 18g
- Carbohydrates: 35g
- Fat: 18g
- Fiber: 5g
- Sugar: 3g

BBQ Chicken Sliders

Difficulty Level: ★★☆☆☆

Total Time: 30 minutes

Servings: 4

Ingredients:

- 2 cups shredded cooked chicken
- 1/2 cup BBQ sauce
- 8 slider buns
- 1 cup coleslaw mix
- 1/4 cup ranch dressing
- 1 tablespoon olive oil
- Salt and pepper to taste

Required Equipment:

- Mixing bowl
- Spoon or spatula
- Grill pan or skillet
- Knife

Preparation:

1. In a mixing bowl, combine the shredded cooked chicken with BBQ sauce. Mix well until the chicken is evenly coated with the sauce.

2. Heat a grill pan or skillet over medium heat and brush it with olive oil.

3. Place the slider buns, cut side down, on the grill pan. Toast them for about 1-2 minutes, or until they are lightly golden. Remove and set aside.

4. In a separate bowl, mix the coleslaw mix with ranch dressing. Season with salt and pepper to taste, and stir until well combined.

5. Assemble the sliders by placing a generous amount of BBQ chicken on the bottom half of each bun.

6. Top the chicken with a heaping tablespoon of the coleslaw mixture.

7. Cover with the top half of the slider buns.

8. Serve immediately, or keep warm in a low oven until ready to serve.

Chef's Tip:
- For a smoky flavor, you can add a teaspoon of liquid smoke to the BBQ chicken mixture.
- If you prefer a crunchier coleslaw, add some chopped nuts or apple slices to the coleslaw mix.
- These sliders can be made ahead of time and assembled just before serving to keep the buns from getting soggy.

Nutritional Information per Serving:
- Calories: 350
- Protein: 22g
- Fat: 15g
- Carbohydrates: 35g
- Fiber: 2g
- Sugar: 12g

Tuna Salad Sandwich

Difficulty Level: ★☆☆☆☆

Total Time: 10 minutes

Servings: 2

Ingredients:

- 1 can (5 oz) tuna in water, drained
- 2 tablespoons mayonnaise
- 1 tablespoon mustard
- 1/4 cup celery, finely chopped
- 1/4 cup red onion, finely chopped
- Salt and pepper, to taste
- 4 slices of whole wheat bread
- Lettuce leaves (optional)
- Tomato slices (optional)

Required Equipment:
- Mixing bowl
- Fork
- Knife
- Spoon

Preparation:

1. In a mixing bowl, use a fork to flake the drained tuna until no large chunks remain.

2. Add mayonnaise and mustard to the tuna. Stir with the fork until the ingredients are well combined.

3. Mix in the finely chopped celery and red onion into the tuna mixture. Season with salt and pepper to taste.

4. Lay out the 4 slices of whole wheat bread. Divide the tuna salad evenly among two slices of bread.

5. If using, add lettuce leaves and tomato slices on top of the tuna salad.

6. Top with the remaining slices of bread to form sandwiches.

7. Use a knife to cut each sandwich in half, if desired.

Chef's Tip:
- For a healthier version, substitute mayonnaise with Greek yogurt or avocado.
- Add a crunch to your sandwich by including sliced cucumbers or apples in the filling.
- To make this sandwich gluten-free, use your favorite gluten-free bread.

Nutritional Information per Serving:
- Calories: 320
- Protein: 25g
- Fat: 9g
- Carbohydrates: 36g
- Fiber: 5g
- Sugar: 5g

Caprese Panini

Difficulty Level: ★☆☆☆☆

Total Time: 15 minutes

Servings: 2

Ingredients:
- 4 slices of sourdough bread
- 2 tablespoons pesto sauce
- 1 large tomato, sliced
- 4 ounces fresh mozzarella cheese, sliced
- 1/4 cup fresh basil leaves
- Salt and pepper, to taste
- 2 tablespoons olive oil

Required Equipment:
- Panini press or grill pan
- Knife
- Spoon or brush for spreading pesto and olive oil

Preparation:

1. Preheat your Panini press or grill pan over medium heat.

2. Spread 1 tablespoon of pesto sauce evenly on one side of each slice of sourdough bread.

3. On two slices of bread, layer the sliced tomatoes, mozzarella cheese, and fresh basil leaves. Season with salt and pepper to taste.

4. Top with the remaining slices of bread, pesto side facing down, to make two sandwiches.

5. Brush the outside of each sandwich lightly with olive oil.

6. Place the sandwiches in the Panini press or on the grill pan. If using a grill pan, press down with a spatula or place a heavy pan on top to press the sandwich down.

7. Grill for about 3-4 minutes on each side or until the bread is toasted and crispy and the cheese has melted.

8. Remove from the press or pan and let sit for 1 minute before cutting each sandwich in half and serving.

Chef's Tip:
- For a variation, add a few slices of cooked chicken breast or swap the pesto for a balsamic glaze for a different flavor profile.
- If you don't have a Panini press, you can make this sandwich in a regular skillet. Just remember to flip it carefully to toast both sides evenly.

- To make this sandwich vegetarian, ensure your pesto is cheese-free or homemade without Parmesan.

Nutritional Information per Serving:
- Calories: 450
- Protein: 22g
- Carbohydrates: 35g
- Fat: 25g
- Sodium: 870mg
- Fiber: 3g

BLT Sandwich

Difficulty Level: ★☆☆☆☆

Total Time: 10 minutes

Servings: 2

Ingredients:
- 4 slices of thick-cut bacon
- 4 slices of bread (sourdough or whole wheat)
- 1 large tomato, sliced
- Lettuce leaves (Romaine or Iceberg)
- 2 tablespoons mayonnaise
- Salt and pepper, to taste

Required Equipment:
- Skillet
- Knife
- Toaster (optional)
- Paper towels
- Spreading knife

Preparation:

1. Heat a skillet over medium heat. Add the bacon slices and cook until crispy, about 3-4 minutes per side. Transfer the bacon to a plate lined with paper towels to drain excess grease.

2. While the bacon is cooking, toast the bread slices to your desired level of crispiness using a toaster or the skillet.

3. Spread 1 tablespoon of mayonnaise on one side of each slice of toasted bread.

4. On two slices of bread, layer the lettuce leaves, followed by tomato slices. Season the tomato slices with a pinch of salt and pepper.

5. Add two slices of cooked bacon on top of the tomatoes for each sandwich.

6. Top the bacon with the remaining slices of bread, mayonnaise side down, to complete the sandwiches.

7. Cut the sandwiches in half, if desired, and serve immediately.

Chef's Tip:
- For a healthier version, try using turkey bacon or a plant-based bacon alternative. You can also use whole grain bread and light mayonnaise.
- Add a slice of avocado or a fried egg to the sandwich for extra flavor and texture.
- If you prefer your lettuce crispy, add it to the sandwich just before serving.

Nutritional Information per Serving:
- Calories: 450
- Protein: 15g
- Carbohydrates: 28g
- Fat: 32g
- Sodium: 870mg
- Fiber: 2g

Greek Salad Wrap

Difficulty Level: ★☆☆☆☆

Total Time: 15 minutes

Servings: 2

Ingredients:
- 2 large whole wheat tortillas
- 1 cup mixed salad greens
- 1/2 cup cherry tomatoes, halved
- 1/4 cup sliced cucumbers
- 1/4 cup red onion, thinly sliced
- 1/4 cup Kalamata olives, pitted and halved
- 1/2 cup feta cheese, crumbled

- 2 tablespoons Greek dressing

- Salt and pepper, to taste

Required Equipment:

- Knife

- Cutting board

- Spoon or small ladle

Preparation:

1. Lay the whole wheat tortillas flat on a clean surface.

2. In the center of each tortilla, evenly distribute the mixed salad greens.

3. Top the greens with cherry tomatoes, sliced cucumbers, red onion, and Kalamata olives.

4. Sprinkle the crumbled feta cheese over the vegetables on each tortilla.

5. Drizzle 1 tablespoon of Greek dressing over the filling of each wrap. Season with salt and pepper to taste.

6. Carefully fold the bottom edge of the tortilla up over the filling. Then, fold in the sides and continue rolling tightly until the wrap is completely sealed.

7. If desired, cut the wrap in half diagonally for easier eating.

Chef's Tip:

- For a protein boost, add grilled chicken or chickpeas to your wrap.

- If you're packing this wrap for lunch, keep the dressing on the side and add it just before eating to keep the tortilla from getting soggy.

- Customize your Greek salad wrap by adding or substituting ingredients based on your preferences. Avocado slices or roasted red peppers make great additions.

Nutritional Information per Serving:

- Calories: 320

- Protein: 10g

- Fat: 18g

- Carbohydrates: 30g

- Fiber: 5g

- Sugar: 5g

Pesto Pasta Salad

Difficulty Level: ★☆☆☆☆

Total Time: 20 minutes

Servings: 4

Ingredients:

- 8 oz fusilli pasta
- 1/2 cup store-bought pesto sauce
- 1 cup cherry tomatoes, halved
- 1/2 cup mozzarella balls (bocconcini), halved
- 1/4 cup pine nuts, toasted
- 1/4 cup fresh basil leaves, torn
- Salt and pepper, to taste
- Grated Parmesan cheese, for garnish

Required Equipment:

- Large pot
- Colander
- Large mixing bowl
- Spoon or spatula
- Skillet (for toasting pine nuts)

Preparation:

1. Bring a large pot of salted water to a boil. Add the fusilli pasta and cook according to package instructions until al dente. Drain the pasta using a colander and rinse under cold water to cool. Set aside.

2. While the pasta is cooking, toast the pine nuts in a dry skillet over medium heat. Stir frequently to prevent burning, until they are golden brown, about 3-4 minutes. Remove from heat and let cool.

3. In a large mixing bowl, combine the cooled pasta, pesto sauce, cherry tomatoes, mozzarella balls, and toasted pine nuts. Toss gently with a spoon or spatula until the pasta is evenly coated with pesto.

4. Season the pasta salad with salt and pepper to taste. Add the torn basil leaves and gently toss again to distribute.

5. Serve the pesto pasta salad in bowls or on plates, garnished with grated Parmesan cheese.

Chef's Tip:

- For a protein boost, consider adding grilled chicken or shrimp to the pasta salad.
- If you prefer a creamier texture, you can mix a tablespoon of mayonnaise or Greek yogurt into the pesto sauce before combining it with the pasta.
- This salad can be served immediately or chilled in the refrigerator for an hour to enhance the flavors.

Nutritional Information per Serving:

- Calories: 380
- Protein: 12g
- Fat: 18g
- Carbohydrates: 42g
- Fiber: 3g
- Sugar: 3g

Spinach and Ricotta Stuffed Pita

Difficulty Level: ★★☆☆☆ (Easy)

Ingredients:

- 1 whole wheat pita bread
- 1/2 cup fresh spinach (chopped)
- 1/4 cup ricotta cheese
- 1 tablespoon olive oil
- Salt and pepper to taste

Instructions:

1. Heat olive oil in a pan and sauté spinach until wilted.
2. Mix the spinach with ricotta cheese in a small bowl. Season with salt and pepper.
3. Slice the pita bread in half and fill each side with the mixture.
4. Heat the stuffed pita in a skillet for 2-3 minutes on each side until warm.

Nutritional Information (per serving):

- Calories: 220
- Protein: 10g
- Carbohydrates: 25g
- Fat: 8g

Mediterranean Chickpea Salad Bowl

Difficulty Level: ★★☆☆☆ (Easy)

Ingredients:

- 1 cup cooked chickpeas
- 1/2 cup cherry tomatoes (halved)
- 1/4 cup cucumber (diced)
- 2 tablespoons crumbled feta cheese
- 1 tablespoon olive oil
- 1 teaspoon lemon juice
- Salt and pepper to taste

Instructions:

1. In a large bowl, combine chickpeas, tomatoes, cucumber, and feta cheese.
2. Drizzle with olive oil and lemon juice.
3. Season with salt and pepper, then toss to mix.

Nutritional Information (per serving):

- Calories: 250
- Protein: 8g
- Carbohydrates: 22g
- Fat: 10g

Sweet Potato and Black Bean Tacos

Difficulty Level: ★★★☆☆ (Moderate)

Ingredients:

- 1 medium sweet potato (diced)
- 1/2 cup canned black beans (rinsed)
- 2 small corn tortillas
- 1 tablespoon olive oil
- 1/4 teaspoon cumin
- 1/4 teaspoon chili powder
- Salt and pepper to taste

Instructions:

1. Preheat oven to 400°F (200°C). Toss sweet potatoes with olive oil, cumin, chili powder, salt, and pepper.
2. Spread sweet potatoes on a baking sheet and roast for 20 minutes or until tender.
3. Warm the tortillas in a skillet.
4. Fill each tortilla with roasted sweet potatoes and black beans.

Nutritional Information (per taco):

- Calories: 180
- Protein: 6g
- Carbohydrates: 28g
- Fat: 5g

Avocado and Egg Salad Wrap

Difficulty Level: ★★☆☆☆ (Easy)

Ingredients:

- 2 large eggs (hard-boiled)
- 1/2 avocado (mashed)
- 1 whole wheat tortilla
- 1 teaspoon lemon juice
- Salt and pepper to taste

Instructions:

1. Mash hard-boiled eggs and avocado in a bowl.
2. Add lemon juice, salt, and pepper, then mix well.
3. Spread the mixture onto the tortilla and roll it up tightly.

Nutritional Information (per serving):

- Calories: 240
- Protein: 10g
- Carbohydrates: 20g
- Fat: 14g

Zucchini Noodles with Pesto

Difficulty Level: ★★★☆☆ (Moderate)

Ingredients:

- 2 medium zucchinis (spiralized)
- 2 tablespoons pesto sauce
- 1 tablespoon olive oil
- 1 tablespoon grated Parmesan cheese
- Salt and pepper to taste

Instructions:

1. Heat olive oil in a large skillet over medium heat.
2. Add zucchini noodles and cook for 2-3 minutes until tender.
3. Remove from heat and toss with pesto sauce.
4. Sprinkle with Parmesan cheese before serving.

Nutritional Information (per serving):

- Calories: 180
- Protein: 5g
- Carbohydrates: 6g
- Fat: 15g

By scanning the QR Code below
you can download 30 Easy Video Recipes

Video Recipes

Chapter 5: Easy Dinner Recipes

Spaghetti Carbonara

Difficulty Level: ★★☆☆

Total Time: 25 minutes

Servings: 4

Ingredients:
- 1 pound spaghetti
- 4 large eggs
- 1 cup freshly grated Parmesan cheese
- 8 slices of bacon, chopped
- 2 cloves garlic, minced
- Salt and black pepper, to taste
- Fresh parsley, chopped (for garnish)

Required Equipment:
- Large pot
- Skillet
- Mixing bowl
- Whisk
- Wooden spoon or spatula

Preparation:

1. Fill a large pot with water and bring it to a boil. Add a pinch of salt and the spaghetti. Cook according to the package instructions until al dente. Reserve 1 cup of pasta water before draining and set the cooked pasta aside.

2. While the pasta is cooking, heat a skillet over medium heat. Add the chopped bacon and cook until crispy, about 5-7 minutes. Add the minced garlic to the bacon during the last 2 minutes of cooking. Remove from heat and set aside.

3. In a mixing bowl, whisk together the eggs and grated Parmesan cheese until well combined. Season with a pinch of salt and black pepper.

4. Return the drained spaghetti to the pot (off heat). Quickly pour the egg and cheese mixture over the hot pasta, stirring vigorously with a wooden spoon or spatula. The heat from the pasta will cook the eggs and melt the cheese, creating a creamy sauce.

5. Add the cooked bacon and garlic to the pasta, mixing well to ensure the bacon is evenly distributed. If the sauce is too thick, slowly add the reserved pasta water, a tablespoon at a time, until the desired consistency is reached.

6. Season with additional salt and black pepper to taste. Garnish with chopped fresh parsley before serving.

Chef's Tip:

- For a vegetarian version, omit the bacon and add sautéed mushrooms or zucchini for a hearty texture.
- Ensure the pasta is hot when adding the egg mixture to help cook the eggs and prevent them from scrambling.
- Serve immediately for the best flavor and texture. Grate additional Parmesan cheese on top for an extra cheesy finish.

Nutritional Information per Serving:

- Calories: 600
- Protein: 25g
- Fat: 25g
- Carbohydrates: 70g
- Fiber: 3g
- Sugar: 3g

Chicken Alfredo Pasta

Difficulty Level: ★★☆☆☆

Total Time: 30 minutes

Servings: 4

Ingredients:
- 8 oz fettuccine pasta
- 2 tablespoons unsalted butter
- 1 cup heavy cream
- 1 clove garlic, minced
- 1 1/2 cups freshly grated Parmesan cheese
- 1/2 teaspoon salt

- 1/4 teaspoon black pepper
- 2 cups cooked, shredded chicken breast
- 2 tablespoons chopped fresh parsley

Required Equipment:
- Large pot
- Colander
- Large skillet
- Wooden spoon or spatula
- Cheese grater

Preparation:

1. Bring a large pot of salted water to a boil. Add fettuccine pasta and cook according to package instructions until al dente. Drain the pasta using a colander and set aside.

2. In the same pot over medium heat, melt the unsalted butter. Add the minced garlic and sauté for 1 minute until fragrant.

3. Pour in the heavy cream and bring to a simmer. Let it cook for 2-3 minutes, stirring occasionally, until the cream starts to thicken.

4. Reduce the heat to low and gradually stir in the freshly grated Parmesan cheese until it melts into the cream, creating a smooth sauce. Season with salt and pepper.

5. Add the cooked, shredded chicken to the sauce and stir to combine. Allow the chicken to warm through for about 2 minutes.

6. Return the cooked fettuccine to the pot and toss with the Alfredo sauce and chicken until the pasta is evenly coated.

7. Serve the Chicken Alfredo Pasta garnished with chopped fresh parsley.

Chef's Tip:
- For a lighter version, substitute half of the heavy cream with whole milk. The sauce will be slightly less thick but still delicious.
- Add a pinch of nutmeg to the Alfredo sauce for a subtle depth of flavor.
- If the sauce thickens too much upon standing, thin it out with a little pasta cooking water until you reach the desired consistency.

Nutritional Information per Serving:
- Calories: 650

- Protein: 35g
- Fat: 48g
- Carbohydrates: 32g
- Fiber: 1g
- Sugar: 3g

Beef Tacos

Difficulty Level: ★☆☆☆☆

Total Time: 30 minutes

Servings: 4

Ingredients:
- 1 lb ground beef
- 8 small corn tortillas
- 1 packet taco seasoning
- 1/2 cup water
- 1 cup shredded lettuce
- 1 tomato, diced
- 1 cup shredded cheddar cheese
- 1/2 cup sour cream
- 1/4 cup salsa
- 1/4 cup diced onions (optional)
- 1/4 cup sliced black olives (optional)

Required Equipment:
- Large skillet
- Measuring cups and spoons
- Knife
- Cutting board
- Spoon or spatula

Preparation:

1. Heat the large skillet over medium-high heat. Add the ground beef to the skillet, breaking it apart with a spoon or spatula. Cook until the beef is thoroughly browned, about 5-7 minutes. Drain any excess fat.

2. Sprinkle the taco seasoning over the cooked beef. Add 1/2 cup water and stir well. Reduce the heat to low and simmer the beef mixture for 5-10 minutes, stirring occasionally, until most of the liquid has been absorbed.

3. While the beef is simmering, prepare the toppings. Dice the tomato and shred the lettuce. Set aside.

4. Warm the corn tortillas in a microwave for 20-30 seconds or in a dry skillet over medium heat for about 15 seconds on each side.

5. To assemble the tacos, place a spoonful of the seasoned beef onto the center of each tortilla. Top with shredded lettuce, diced tomato, shredded cheddar cheese, and a dollop of sour cream. Add salsa, diced onions, and sliced black olives if desired.

6. Fold the tortillas in half around the fillings. Serve immediately.

Chef's Tip:
- For a vegetarian option, substitute ground beef with a mix of black beans and quinoa. Adjust the cooking time accordingly.
- Add a squeeze of lime juice and a sprinkle of fresh chopped cilantro to each taco for extra flavor.
- If you like your tacos spicy, mix in some diced jalapeños with the beef or top your tacos with hot sauce.

Nutritional Information per Serving:
- Calories: 450
- Protein: 25g
- Fat: 25g
- Carbohydrates: 35g
- Fiber: 5g
- Sugar: 3g

Veggie Stir-Fry

Difficulty Level: ★☆☆☆☆

Total Time: 20 minutes

Servings: 4

Ingredients:
- 2 tablespoons vegetable oil
- 1 cup broccoli florets
- 1 cup sliced carrots

- 1 red bell pepper, julienned
- 1 cup snap peas
- 1/2 cup sliced mushrooms
- 2 cloves garlic, minced
- 1 tablespoon soy sauce
- 1 tablespoon oyster sauce (optional, can substitute with more soy sauce for a vegetarian option)
- 1 teaspoon sesame oil
- Salt and pepper, to taste
- Cooked rice or noodles, for serving

Required Equipment:
- Large skillet or wok
- Wooden spoon or spatula
- Knife
- Cutting board
- Measuring spoons

Preparation:

1. Heat the vegetable oil in a large skillet or wok over medium-high heat.

2. Add the broccoli and carrots to the skillet. Stir-fry for about 3 minutes, or until they start to soften.

3. Add the red bell pepper, snap peas, and mushrooms to the skillet. Continue to stir-fry for another 2 minutes.

4. Stir in the minced garlic and cook for about 30 seconds, until fragrant.

5. Pour the soy sauce, oyster sauce (if using), and sesame oil over the vegetables. Stir well to combine and coat the vegetables in the sauces. Season with salt and pepper to taste.

6. Cook for an additional 2 minutes, or until all the vegetables are tender but still crisp.

7. Serve the veggie stir-fry hot over cooked rice or noodles.

Chef's Tip:
- Feel free to swap out or add any vegetables you have on hand. This recipe is great for using up leftover veggies in the fridge.
- For a spicy kick, add a drizzle of sriracha or a sprinkle of red pepper flakes when adding the sauces.
- To make this dish a complete meal, consider adding tofu, chicken, or shrimp for added protein. Just cook the protein first, remove it from the skillet, then add it back in with the sauces to reheat.

Nutritional Information per Serving:

- Calories: 120

- Protein: 3g

- Fat: 7g

- Carbohydrates: 12g

- Fiber: 3g

- Sugar: 5g

Lemon Herb Grilled Chicken

Difficulty Level: ★★☆☆☆

Total Time: 25 minutes

Servings: 4

Ingredients:

- 4 boneless, skinless chicken breasts

- 2 tablespoons olive oil

- 2 tablespoons fresh lemon juice

- 1 tablespoon chopped fresh rosemary

- 1 tablespoon chopped fresh thyme

- 2 cloves garlic, minced

- Salt and pepper, to taste

- Lemon slices and additional fresh herbs for garnish

Required Equipment:

- Grill or grill pan

- Mixing bowl

- Whisk

- Measuring spoons

- Garlic press (optional)

- Tongs

Preparation:

1. Preheat your grill or grill pan over medium-high heat.

2. In a mixing bowl, whisk together olive oil, lemon juice, rosemary, thyme, and minced garlic to create the marinade.

3. Season both sides of the chicken breasts with salt and pepper.

4. Place the chicken in the bowl with the marinade, ensuring each piece is well coated. Let it marinate for at least 10 minutes, or up to 30 minutes if time allows.

5. Using tongs, remove the chicken from the marinade and place it on the hot grill. Discard any leftover marinade.

6. Grill the chicken for 6-7 minutes on each side, or until the internal temperature reaches 165°F (74°C) and the juices run clear.

7. Once cooked, transfer the chicken to a plate and let it rest for a few minutes.

8. Serve the grilled chicken garnished with lemon slices and a sprinkle of fresh herbs.

Chef's Tip:

- For an even juicier chicken, pound the breasts to an even thickness before marinating. This helps them cook more evenly and retain moisture.

- If you don't have fresh herbs, you can substitute with 1 teaspoon each of dried rosemary and thyme.

- To prevent sticking, make sure your grill is clean and properly oiled before cooking the chicken.

- For a complete meal, serve the chicken with a side of grilled vegetables or a fresh garden salad.

Nutritional Information per Serving:

- Calories: 220
- Protein: 26g
- Fat: 12g
- Carbohydrates: 2g
- Sodium: 70mg
- Fiber: 0g

Shrimp Scampi

Difficulty Level: ★★☆☆☆

Total Time: 25 minutes

Servings: 4

Ingredients:
- 1 pound large shrimp, peeled and deveined
- 8 ounces linguine pasta
- 2 tablespoons unsalted butter
- 2 tablespoons olive oil
- 4 cloves garlic, minced
- 1/2 teaspoon red pepper flakes (optional)
- 1/2 cup chicken broth

- Juice of 1 lemon
- Zest of 1 lemon
- 1/4 cup freshly chopped parsley
- Salt and pepper, to taste
- Grated Parmesan cheese, for serving

Required Equipment:
- Large pot
- Colander
- Large skillet
- Measuring cups and spoons
- Knife
- Cutting board

Preparation:

1. Bring a large pot of salted water to a boil. Add the linguine and cook according to package instructions until al dente. Drain the pasta in a colander and set aside.

2. While the pasta is cooking, heat the butter and olive oil in a large skillet over medium heat.

3. Add the minced garlic and red pepper flakes to the skillet. Sauté for 1-2 minutes, or until the garlic is fragrant but not browned.

4. Increase the heat to medium-high and add the shrimp to the skillet. Season with salt and pepper. Cook for 2-3 minutes on each side, or until the shrimp are pink and opaque.

5. Remove the shrimp from the skillet and set aside. In the same skillet, add the chicken broth and lemon juice. Bring to a simmer and let it reduce slightly, about 2-3 minutes.

6. Return the shrimp to the skillet. Add the cooked linguine, lemon zest, and chopped parsley. Toss everything together until the pasta is well coated with the sauce and the shrimp are evenly distributed.

7. Serve the shrimp scampi immediately, garnished with grated Parmesan cheese.

Chef's Tip:
- For an extra touch of flavor, finish the dish with a drizzle of high-quality extra virgin olive oil just before serving.
- If you prefer a spicier dish, increase the amount of red pepper flakes according to your taste.
- To make this dish more colorful and nutritious, consider adding a handful of spinach or cherry tomatoes when adding the shrimp back to the skillet.

Nutritional Information per Serving:

- Calories: 450

- Protein: 28g

- Fat: 18g

- Carbohydrates: 45g

- Fiber: 2g

- Sugar: 2g

BBQ Pulled Pork Sandwiches

Difficulty Level: ★★☆☆☆

Total Time: 6 hours 15 minutes

Servings: 8

Ingredients:

- 2 pounds pork shoulder

- 1 tablespoon salt

- 1/2 tablespoon black pepper

- 1 tablespoon smoked paprika

- 2 cups BBQ sauce, divided

- 1/2 cup apple cider vinegar

- 1/4 cup honey

- 1/4 cup brown sugar

- 2 cloves garlic, minced

- 8 hamburger buns

- Coleslaw (optional, for serving)

Required Equipment:

- Slow cooker

- Forks (for shredding)

- Measuring cups and spoons

- Small bowl

Preparation:

1. Mix salt, black pepper, and smoked paprika in a small bowl. Rub this mixture all over the pork shoulder, ensuring it's fully coated.

2. Place the seasoned pork shoulder in the slow cooker.

3. In a separate bowl, combine 1 cup of BBQ sauce, apple cider vinegar, honey, brown sugar, and minced garlic. Stir well to combine.

4. Pour the BBQ sauce mixture over the pork shoulder in the slow cooker.

5. Cover and cook on low for 6 hours or until the pork is very tender and falls apart easily when prodded with a fork.

6. Once cooked, transfer the pork shoulder to a large plate or cutting board. Using two forks, shred the meat into bite-sized pieces, discarding any fat or gristle.

7. Return the shredded pork to the slow cooker and mix with the remaining juices. Stir in the remaining 1 cup of BBQ sauce until well combined.

8. Increase the slow cooker's heat to high and cook the shredded pork for an additional 15 minutes, or until heated through and the sauce is bubbly.

9. Toast the hamburger buns lightly, if desired.

10. Serve the BBQ pulled pork on the toasted buns, topped with coleslaw if using.

Chef's Tip:
- For a smokier flavor, you can add a teaspoon of liquid smoke to the BBQ sauce mixture.
- If the sauce is too thin after shredding the pork, you can remove the lid and cook on high for 30-45 minutes to thicken.
- Customize your sandwich with additional toppings like pickles, sliced onions, or jalapeños for an extra kick.

Nutritional Information per Serving:
- Calories: 560
- Protein: 35g
- Fat: 20g
- Carbohydrates: 65g
- Fiber: 2g
- Sugar: 35g

Margherita Pizza

Difficulty Level: ★☆☆☆☆

Total Time: 30 minutes

Servings: 4

Ingredients:
- 1 pound pizza dough (store-bought or homemade)
- 1/2 cup tomato sauce
- 2 cups shredded mozzarella cheese
- 2 large tomatoes, thinly sliced
- 1/4 cup fresh basil leaves
- 1 tablespoon olive oil
- Salt and pepper, to taste

Required Equipment:
- Oven
- Baking sheet or pizza stone
- Rolling pin (if using a baking sheet)
- Knife
- Spoon

Preparation:

1. Preheat your oven to 475°F (245°C). If using a pizza stone, place it in the oven now to preheat. If using a baking sheet, lightly grease it with olive oil.

2. On a lightly floured surface, roll out the pizza dough to about 12 inches in diameter. Transfer the dough to the preheated pizza stone or prepared baking sheet.

3. Spread the tomato sauce evenly over the pizza dough, leaving a small border around the edges.

4. Sprinkle the shredded mozzarella cheese over the tomato sauce.

5. Arrange the thinly sliced tomatoes on top of the cheese. Season with salt and pepper.

6. Drizzle the tablespoon of olive oil over the top of the pizza.

7. Bake in the preheated oven for 12-15 minutes, or until the crust is golden brown and the cheese is bubbly and slightly browned.

8. Remove the pizza from the oven and immediately top with fresh basil leaves.

9. Let the pizza cool for a few minutes before slicing and serving.

Chef's Tip:

- For a crispier crust, pre-bake the pizza dough for 5-7 minutes before adding the toppings.

- Feel free to add a sprinkle of red pepper flakes if you enjoy a little heat.

- If you have a pizza peel, use it to easily transfer the pizza to and from the oven, especially if using a pizza stone.

Nutritional Information per Serving:

- Calories: 380

- Protein: 18g

- Fat: 15g

- Carbohydrates: 45g

- Fiber: 2g

- Sugar: 5g

Teriyaki Chicken Bowls

Difficulty Level: ★★☆☆☆

Total Time: 30 minutes

Servings: 4

Ingredients:

- 1 lb boneless, skinless chicken breasts, cut into bite-sized pieces

- 1/4 cup soy sauce

- 2 tablespoons honey

- 1 tablespoon rice vinegar

- 1 teaspoon sesame oil

- 1 teaspoon grated ginger

- 2 cloves garlic, minced

- 1 tablespoon cornstarch

- 2 tablespoons water

- 2 cups cooked white rice

- 1 cup broccoli florets, steamed

- 1 tablespoon sesame seeds

- 2 green onions, thinly sliced

Required Equipment:

- Large skillet or wok

- Small bowl

- Measuring cups and spoons

- Knife
- Cutting board
- Spoon or spatula

Preparation:

1. In a large skillet or wok, heat the sesame oil over medium-high heat. Add the chicken pieces and cook until they are browned and cooked through, about 5-7 minutes. Remove the chicken from the skillet and set aside.

2. In the same skillet, add the grated ginger and minced garlic. Sauté for about 1 minute, or until fragrant.

3. In a small bowl, whisk together the soy sauce, honey, rice vinegar, and cornstarch with 2 tablespoons of water until smooth.

4. Pour the soy sauce mixture into the skillet with the ginger and garlic. Bring to a simmer and cook for 2-3 minutes, or until the sauce thickens.

5. Return the cooked chicken to the skillet and toss to coat with the sauce. Cook for an additional 2 minutes to ensure the chicken is heated through and coated well.

6. Divide the cooked white rice among four bowls. Top each bowl with an equal portion of the teriyaki chicken and steamed broccoli florets.

7. Garnish each bowl with sesame seeds and sliced green onions before serving.

Chef's Tip:
- For a spicier version, add a dash of sriracha or chili flakes to the teriyaki sauce.
- Feel free to substitute the broccoli with other vegetables like bell peppers, snap peas, or carrots for a colorful and nutritious twist.
- If you prefer a thicker sauce, you can adjust the amount of cornstarch to your liking. Just remember to dissolve it in water before adding to prevent clumping.

Nutritional Information per Serving:
- Calories: 350
- Protein: 28g
- Fat: 6g
- Carbohydrates: 46g
- Fiber: 2g
- Sugar: 9g

Baked Ziti

Difficulty Level: ★★☆☆☆

Total Time: 45 minutes

Servings: 6

Ingredients:
- 1 lb ziti pasta
- 24 oz marinara sauce
- 1 cup ricotta cheese
- 2 cups shredded mozzarella cheese
- 1/2 cup grated Parmesan cheese
- 1 egg, beaten
- 1 teaspoon dried oregano
- 1 teaspoon garlic powder
- Salt and pepper, to taste
- Fresh basil leaves, for garnish

Required Equipment:
- Large pot
- Colander
- Mixing bowl
- 9x13 inch baking dish
- Spoon or spatula

Preparation:

1. Preheat your oven to 375°F (190°C).

2. Cook the ziti pasta in a large pot of boiling salted water according to package instructions for al dente. Drain the pasta using a colander and set aside.

3. In a mixing bowl, combine the ricotta cheese, 1 cup of mozzarella cheese, Parmesan cheese, beaten egg, dried oregano, garlic powder, salt, and pepper. Mix well until all ingredients are evenly incorporated.

4. In the 9x13 inch baking dish, spread a thin layer of marinara sauce to cover the bottom.

5. Add half of the cooked ziti pasta over the sauce in an even layer.

6. Spread half of the cheese mixture over the pasta, then top with half of the remaining marinara sauce.

7. Repeat the layers with the remaining pasta, cheese mixture, and marinara sauce.

8. Sprinkle the remaining 1 cup of mozzarella cheese evenly over the top.

9. Cover the baking dish with aluminum foil and bake in the preheated oven for 25 minutes.

10. Remove the foil and continue baking for an additional 10 minutes, or until the cheese is bubbly and slightly golden.

11. Let the baked ziti cool for 5 minutes before garnishing with fresh basil leaves. Serve warm.

Chef's Tip:

- For a meatier version, brown 1/2 lb of ground beef or Italian sausage and add it to the marinara sauce before layering.
- If you prefer a creamier texture, you can add an extra 1/2 cup of ricotta cheese to the cheese mixture.
- Leftovers can be stored in an airtight container in the refrigerator for up to 3 days and reheated in the oven or microwave.

Nutritional Information per Serving:

- Calories: 450
- Protein: 25g
- Fat: 20g
- Carbohydrates: 45g
- Fiber: 3g
- Sugar: 5g

Garlic Butter Salmon with Asparagus

Difficulty Level: ★★☆☆☆ (Easy)

Ingredients:

- 2 salmon fillets
- 1 bunch asparagus (trimmed)
- 2 tablespoons butter (melted)
- 2 garlic cloves (minced)
- 1 teaspoon lemon juice
- Salt and pepper to taste

Instructions:

1. Preheat oven to 375°F (190°C). Line a baking sheet with parchment paper.

2. Place salmon fillets and asparagus on the baking sheet.
3. In a small bowl, mix melted butter, garlic, and lemon juice. Drizzle over salmon and asparagus.
4. Bake for 12-15 minutes, or until salmon is cooked through and flakes easily.

Nutritional Information (per serving):

- Calories: 320
- Protein: 30g
- Carbohydrates: 5g
- Fat: 20g

Stuffed Bell Peppers

Difficulty Level: ★★★☆☆ (Moderate)

Ingredients:

- 4 bell peppers (tops removed, seeds removed)
- 1/2 pound ground turkey or beef
- 1 cup cooked rice
- 1/2 cup diced tomatoes
- 1/4 cup shredded cheddar cheese
- 1 tablespoon olive oil
- Salt and pepper to taste

Instructions:

1. Preheat oven to 375°F (190°C).
2. Heat olive oil in a skillet over medium heat. Cook ground meat until browned, then mix in rice and diced tomatoes.
3. Stuff each bell pepper with the mixture and place in a baking dish.
4. Sprinkle with cheese and bake for 20 minutes.

Nutritional Information (per stuffed pepper):

- Calories: 250
- Protein: 18g
- Carbohydrates: 20g
- Fat: 10g

Creamy Tomato Basil Soup with Grilled Cheese

Difficulty Level: ★★☆☆☆ (Easy)

Ingredients:

- 1 can (14 oz) diced tomatoes
- 1/2 cup heavy cream
- 1/2 teaspoon dried basil
- 1 cup vegetable broth
- 2 slices whole-grain bread
- 2 slices cheddar cheese
- 1 tablespoon butter

Instructions:

1. In a pot, combine diced tomatoes, vegetable broth, and basil. Simmer for 10 minutes.
2. Blend the mixture until smooth, then stir in heavy cream. Simmer for another 5 minutes.
3. For the grilled cheese, butter one side of each bread slice, place cheese between, and grill in a pan until golden brown.
4. Serve soup with grilled cheese for dipping.

Nutritional Information (per serving):

- Calories: 400
- Protein: 10g
- Carbohydrates: 30g
- Fat: 25g

Honey Garlic Chicken Thighs

Difficulty Level: ★★☆☆☆ (Easy)

Ingredients:

- 4 chicken thighs (bone-in, skin-on)
- 2 tablespoons honey
- 2 garlic cloves (minced)
- 1 tablespoon soy sauce
- 1 tablespoon olive oil
- Salt and pepper to taste

Instructions:

1. Preheat oven to 400°F (200°C).
2. In a small bowl, mix honey, garlic, soy sauce, and olive oil.
3. Place chicken thighs on a baking sheet and brush with the honey mixture.
4. Bake for 25-30 minutes, or until the internal temperature reaches 165°F (74°C).

Nutritional Information (per serving):

- Calories: 310
- Protein: 25g
- Carbohydrates: 8g
- Fat: 20g

Spinach and Mushroom Pasta

Difficulty Level: ★★★☆☆ (Moderate)

Ingredients:

- 8 oz penne pasta
- 1 cup fresh spinach
- 1 cup mushrooms (sliced)
- 1/2 cup heavy cream
- 1/4 cup grated Parmesan cheese
- 1 tablespoon olive oil
- Salt and pepper to taste

Instructions:

1. Cook pasta according to package instructions and set aside.
2. Heat olive oil in a pan and sauté mushrooms until tender. Add spinach and cook until wilted.
3. Stir in heavy cream and Parmesan cheese, cooking until sauce thickens.
4. Toss pasta with the sauce and serve warm.

Nutritional Information (per serving):

- Calories: 350
- Protein: 12g
- Carbohydrates: 45g
- Fat: 15g

Chapter 6: Dessert Recipes

Chocolate Chip Cookies

Difficulty Level: ★☆☆☆

Total Time: 22 minutes

Servings: 24 cookies

Ingredients:

- 2 1/4 cups all-purpose flour
- 1/2 teaspoon baking soda
- 1 cup unsalted butter, room temperature
- 1/2 cup granulated sugar
- 1 cup packed light-brown sugar
- 1 teaspoon salt
- 2 teaspoons pure vanilla extract
- 2 large eggs
- 2 cups semisweet and/or milk chocolate chips

Required Equipment:

- Large mixing bowl
- Medium mixing bowl
- Electric mixer or whisk
- Baking sheet
- Parchment paper
- Cooling rack

Preparation:

1. Preheat your oven to 350°F (175°C). Line a baking sheet with parchment paper.

2. In a medium mixing bowl, whisk together the all-purpose flour and baking soda. Set aside.

3. In a large mixing bowl, use an electric mixer to cream the unsalted butter, granulated sugar, light-brown sugar, and salt until the mixture is light and fluffy. This should take about 3 minutes.

4. Beat in the pure vanilla extract and eggs, one at a time, ensuring each egg is fully incorporated before adding the next.

5. Gradually add the flour mixture to the wet ingredients, beating on low speed just until the flour is mixed in.

6. Stir in the chocolate chips with a wooden spoon or spatula.

7. Drop tablespoon-sized balls of dough onto the prepared baking sheet, spacing them about 2 inches apart.

8. Bake in the preheated oven for 8-10 minutes, or until the edges are golden but the centers are still soft.

9. Remove from the oven and let the cookies cool on the baking sheet for 2 minutes. Then transfer them to a cooling rack to cool completely.

Chef's Tip:

- For chewier cookies, try baking at a lower temperature (325°F or 163°C) for a slightly longer time (10-12 minutes).
- Experiment with adding nuts, such as chopped walnuts or pecans, for added texture and flavor.
- If you prefer your cookies with less spread, chill the dough for 30 minutes before baking.

Nutritional Information per Serving:

- Calories: 210
- Fat: 11g
- Saturated Fat: 7g
- Cholesterol: 35mg
- Sodium: 85mg
- Carbohydrates: 29g
- Fiber: 1g
- Sugar: 20g
- Protein: 2g

Red Velvet Cupcakes

Difficulty Level: ★★☆☆☆

Total Time: 35 minutes

Servings: 12 cupcakes

Ingredients:

- 1 1/4 cups all-purpose flour
- 1 cup granulated sugar
- 1/2 cup unsweetened cocoa powder
- 1/2 teaspoon baking soda
- 1/4 teaspoon salt
- 3/4 cup buttermilk
- 1/3 cup vegetable oil
- 1 large egg
- 2 teaspoons red food coloring
- 1 teaspoon vanilla extract
- 1 teaspoon white vinegar

For the Cream Cheese Frosting:

- 1/2 cup unsalted butter, softened
- 8 oz cream cheese, softened
- 4 cups powdered sugar
- 1 teaspoon vanilla extract

Required Equipment:

- Cupcake tin
- Cupcake liners
- Mixing bowls
- Electric mixer
- Measuring cups and spoons
- Toothpick
- Cooling rack

Preparation:

1. Preheat your oven to 350°F (175°C). Line a cupcake tin with cupcake liners.

2. In a large mixing bowl, whisk together the flour, granulated sugar, cocoa powder, baking soda, and salt.

3. In another mixing bowl, combine the buttermilk, vegetable oil, egg, red food coloring, vanilla extract, and white vinegar. Beat with an electric mixer on medium speed until smooth.

4. Gradually add the wet ingredients to the dry ingredients, mixing on low speed until just combined. Do not overmix.

5. Fill each cupcake liner about two-thirds full with the batter.

6. Bake for 18-20 minutes, or until a toothpick inserted into the center of a cupcake comes out clean.

7. Remove the cupcakes from the oven and allow them to cool in the tin for 5 minutes before transferring them to a cooling rack to cool completely.

For the Cream Cheese Frosting:

8. In a large mixing bowl, beat the softened butter and cream cheese with an electric mixer on medium speed until smooth.

9. Gradually add the powdered sugar, 1 cup at a time, beating on low speed until combined. Stir in the vanilla extract.

10. Once the cupcakes are completely cooled, frost them with the cream cheese frosting using a knife or piping bag.

Chef's Tip:

- For a smoother frosting, make sure the butter and cream cheese are at room temperature before mixing.
- If the cupcake batter is too thick, add a tablespoon more of buttermilk to achieve the desired consistency.
- To make your cupcakes extra festive, sprinkle some red sugar crystals or red velvet cake crumbs on top of the frosting.

Nutritional Information per Serving:

- Calories: 420
- Fat: 20g
- Saturated Fat: 8g
- Cholesterol: 55mg
- Sodium: 180mg
- Carbohydrates: 58g
- Fiber: 1g
- Sugar: 48g
- Protein: 4g

Lemon Bars

Difficulty Level: ★☆☆☆☆

Total Time: 50 minutes

Servings: 16 bars

Ingredients:

- 1 cup all-purpose flour
- 1/4 cup powdered sugar, plus more for dusting
- 1/2 cup unsalted butter, cold and cubed
- 2 large eggs
- 1 cup granulated sugar
- 2 tablespoons all-purpose flour
- 1/4 cup fresh lemon juice
- 1 tablespoon lemon zest

Required Equipment:

- 8x8 inch baking pan
- Parchment paper
- Mixing bowls (2)
- Whisk
- Sifter or fine mesh strainer

Preparation:

1. Preheat your oven to 350°F (175°C). Line the 8x8 inch baking pan with parchment paper, leaving an overhang on the sides for easy removal.

2. In a mixing bowl, combine 1 cup flour and 1/4 cup powdered sugar. Add the cold, cubed butter. Use your fingers or a pastry cutter to blend the ingredients until the mixture resembles coarse crumbs.

3. Press the crumb mixture firmly into the bottom of the prepared baking pan. Bake in the preheated oven for 20 minutes, or until lightly golden.

4. While the crust is baking, prepare the lemon filling. In a separate bowl, whisk together the eggs and granulated sugar until smooth. Stir in 2 tablespoons of flour, lemon juice, and lemon zest until well combined.

5. Pour the lemon filling over the hot crust as soon as it comes out of the oven.

6. Return the pan to the oven and bake for an additional 20-25 minutes, or until the filling is set and no longer jiggles.

7. Remove from the oven and let cool completely in the pan on a wire rack. Once cooled, use the parchment paper overhang to lift the lemon bars out of the pan. Cut into 16 squares.

8. Dust the tops of the lemon bars with additional powdered sugar before serving.

Chef's Tip:

- For a smoother top, sift the powdered sugar over the bars through a fine mesh strainer.
- If you prefer a more tart flavor, increase the lemon juice to 1/3 cup and adjust the flour in the filling to 3 tablespoons to compensate for the extra liquid.
- Store leftover lemon bars in an airtight container in the refrigerator for up to 5 days. Allow them to come to room temperature before serving for the best flavor.

Nutritional Information per Serving:

- Calories: 150
- Fat: 6g
- Saturated Fat: 3.5g
- Cholesterol: 40mg
- Sodium: 15mg
- Carbohydrates: 22g
- Fiber: 0g
- Sugar: 15g
- Protein: 2g

Brownie Sundaes

Difficulty Level: ★☆☆☆☆

Total Time: 25 minutes

Servings: 4

Ingredients:

- 1 pint vanilla ice cream
- 4 brownies (store-bought or homemade, approximately 2-inch squares)
- 1/2 cup chocolate syrup
- 1/4 cup whipped cream
- 1/4 cup chopped nuts (optional, such as pecans or walnuts)
- 4 cherries for garnish

Required Equipment:

- 4 serving bowls or glasses

- Ice cream scoop
- Spoon

Preparation:

1. If using homemade brownies, ensure they have cooled completely before starting the assembly. For store-bought brownies, remove them from packaging and cut into 2-inch squares if not already sized.

2. Place one brownie at the bottom of each serving bowl or glass.

3. Using an ice cream scoop, place one generous scoop of vanilla ice cream on top of each brownie.

4. Drizzle each serving with 2 tablespoons of chocolate syrup, ensuring even coverage over the ice cream.

5. Add a dollop of whipped cream on top of the ice cream for each sundae.

6. If using, sprinkle each sundae with 1 tablespoon of chopped nuts for added texture and flavor.

7. Top each sundae with a cherry for a classic finish.

8. Serve immediately, allowing each person to dig in and enjoy the layers of their brownie sundae.

Chef's Tip:

- For a warm brownie experience, briefly microwave each brownie for about 10-15 seconds before placing it in the serving bowl. The contrast of warm brownie and cold ice cream makes for a delightful treat.
- Feel free to customize your sundae with different ice cream flavors or additional toppings like sprinkles, caramel sauce, or fresh fruit.
- To make this dessert ahead of time, prepare the brownies and store them at room temperature. Assemble the sundaes just before serving to ensure the ice cream doesn't melt.

Nutritional Information per Serving:

- Calories: 450 (varies depending on brownie and toppings used)
- Fat: 20g
- Saturated Fat: 9g
- Cholesterol: 45mg
- Sodium: 220mg
- Carbohydrates: 60g
- Fiber: 2g
- Sugar: 45g
- Protein: 5g

Strawberry Shortcake

Difficulty Level: ★☆☆☆☆

Total Time: 1 hour 20 minutes

Servings: 6

Ingredients:

- 1 quart strawberries, hulled and sliced
- 1/4 cup granulated sugar
- 2 cups all-purpose flour
- 4 teaspoons baking powder
- 1/2 teaspoon salt
- 1/4 cup cold unsalted butter, cubed
- 2/3 cup whole milk
- 1 cup heavy whipping cream
- 2 tablespoons powdered sugar
- 1 teaspoon vanilla extract

Required Equipment:

- Large mixing bowl
- Medium mixing bowl
- Baking sheet
- Parchment paper
- Electric mixer or whisk
- Knife
- Oven

Preparation:

1. Preheat your oven to 425°F (220°C). Line a baking sheet with parchment paper.

2. In a large mixing bowl, combine the strawberries and granulated sugar. Stir gently and set aside for about 30 minutes to allow the strawberries to release their juices.

3. In a medium mixing bowl, whisk together the flour, baking powder, and salt. Add the cubed butter and use your fingers or a pastry cutter to blend the butter into the flour mixture until it resembles coarse crumbs.

4. Gradually stir in the milk until the dough comes together. Be careful not to overmix.

5. Turn the dough out onto a lightly floured surface and gently pat it into a 1-inch thick rectangle. Use a knife to cut the dough into 6 equal squares or rounds.

6. Place the dough pieces on the prepared baking sheet and bake for 12-15 minutes, or until they are golden brown. Remove from the oven and let cool on a wire rack.

7. While the shortcakes are cooling, use an electric mixer to beat the heavy whipping cream, powdered sugar, and vanilla extract in a medium bowl until stiff peaks form.

8. To assemble, split each shortcake in half horizontally. Spoon a generous amount of the sugared strawberries and their juice onto the bottom half of each shortcake. Top with a dollop of whipped cream and then cover with the top half of the shortcake.

9. Serve immediately.

Chef's Tip:

- For an extra burst of flavor, you can add a splash of orange liqueur or a teaspoon of orange zest to the strawberries when mixing them with the granulated sugar.
- If you prefer a sweeter shortcake, you can increase the granulated sugar in the dough to 1/3 cup.
- The shortcakes can be made a day in advance and stored in an airtight container at room temperature. Assemble with strawberries and whipped cream just before serving.

Nutritional Information per Serving:

- Calories: 450
- Fat: 26g
- Saturated Fat: 16g
- Cholesterol: 85mg
- Sodium: 310mg
- Carbohydrates: 48g
- Fiber: 2g
- Sugar: 18g
- Protein: 6g

Apple Pie

Difficulty Level: ★★☆☆☆

Total Time: 1 hour 30 minutes

Servings: 8

Ingredients:

- 2 1/2 cups all-purpose flour, plus extra for rolling
- 1 cup unsalted butter, chilled and diced
- 1/2 teaspoon salt
- 1/2 cup ice water
- 6 cups thinly sliced apples (about 6 medium apples, a mix of Granny Smith and Honeycrisp is recommended)
- 3/4 cup sugar
- 2 tablespoons all-purpose flour
- 1/2 teaspoon ground cinnamon
- 1/4 teaspoon ground nutmeg
- 1 tablespoon lemon juice
- 1 egg yolk
- 1 tablespoon water
- Additional sugar for sprinkling

Required Equipment:

- Mixing bowls
- Pie dish (9-inch)
- Rolling pin
- Pastry brush

Preparation:

1. In a large mixing bowl, combine 2 1/2 cups flour and 1/2 teaspoon salt. Cut in the chilled butter until the mixture resembles coarse crumbs. Gradually add ice water, stirring with a fork, until a dough forms. Divide dough in half, shape into discs, wrap in plastic, and refrigerate for at least 30 minutes.

2. Preheat oven to 425°F (220°C).

3. On a lightly floured surface, roll out one dough disc into a 12-inch circle. Transfer to a 9-inch pie dish, gently pressing into the bottom and sides. Trim excess dough from the edges.

4. In a large bowl, combine sliced apples, 3/4 cup sugar, 2 tablespoons flour, cinnamon, nutmeg, and lemon juice. Toss to coat apples evenly.

5. Fill the prepared pie crust with the apple mixture, mounding slightly in the center.

6. Roll out the second dough disc on a floured surface into a 12-inch circle. Place over the filling. Trim, seal, and crimp the edges. Cut slits in the top crust to allow steam to escape.

7. Beat the egg yolk with 1 tablespoon water. Brush the mixture over the top crust and edges. Sprinkle with additional sugar.

8. Bake in the preheated oven for 45-50 minutes, or until the crust is golden brown and filling is bubbly. If the edges brown too quickly, cover them with foil.

9. Remove from oven and cool on a wire rack before serving.

Chef's Tip:

- For a shiny, golden crust, brush the top crust with a mixture of egg yolk and water before baking.
- If you prefer a sweeter pie, increase the sugar in the filling to 1 cup.
- Serve the apple pie with a scoop of vanilla ice cream or a dollop of whipped cream for an extra special treat.

Nutritional Information per Serving:

- Calories: 410
- Fat: 22g
- Saturated Fat: 14g
- Cholesterol: 80mg
- Sodium: 150mg
- Carbohydrates: 50g
- Fiber: 3g
- Sugar: 25g
- Protein: 4g

Cheesecake Bites

Difficulty Level: ★☆☆☆☆

Total Time: 2 hours 30 minutes (includes chilling time)

Servings: 24 bites

Ingredients:

- 1 cup graham cracker crumbs
- 4 tablespoons unsalted butter, melted
- 2 tablespoons sugar
- 1 package (8 oz) cream cheese, softened
- 1/4 cup powdered sugar

- 1 teaspoon vanilla extract
- 1/2 cup heavy cream
- 1/4 cup strawberry jam

Required Equipment:

- Mixing bowls
- Hand mixer or stand mixer
- Measuring cups and spoons
- Mini muffin tin
- Mini muffin liners
- Spoon
- Refrigerator

Preparation:

1. Line a mini muffin tin with mini muffin liners.
2. In a mixing bowl, combine graham cracker crumbs, melted butter, and sugar. Mix until well combined.
3. Press about a teaspoon of the graham cracker mixture into the bottom of each muffin liner to form a crust. Press down firmly to compact. Place in the refrigerator to chill while preparing the filling.
4. In another mixing bowl, beat the softened cream cheese, powdered sugar, and vanilla extract with a hand mixer or stand mixer until smooth and creamy.
5. In a separate bowl, whip the heavy cream until stiff peaks form. Gently fold the whipped cream into the cream cheese mixture until well combined.
6. Spoon or pipe the cream cheese mixture onto the graham cracker crusts in the muffin liners, filling nearly to the top.
7. Place a small dollop (about 1/2 teaspoon) of strawberry jam on top of each cheesecake bite. Use a toothpick to swirl the jam into the cream cheese mixture slightly.
8. Chill the cheesecake bites in the refrigerator for at least 2 hours, or until set.
9. Once set, remove the cheesecake bites from the muffin tin and serve.

Chef's Tip:

- For a fun variation, try using different flavors of jam like raspberry, blueberry, or apricot.
- Ensure the cream cheese is at room temperature before mixing to avoid lumps in your cheesecake filling.
- These cheesecake bites can be made ahead of time and stored in the refrigerator for up to 3 days.

Nutritional Information per Serving:

- Calories: 120
- Fat: 8g

- Saturated Fat: 5g
- Cholesterol: 25mg
- Sodium: 80mg
- Carbohydrates: 10g
- Fiber: 0g
- Sugar: 7g
- Protein: 1g

Chocolate Mousse

Difficulty Level: ★☆☆☆☆

Total Time: 20 minutes

Servings: 4

Ingredients:

- 8 oz semi-sweet chocolate chips
- 2 cups heavy cream, divided
- 1/4 cup granulated sugar
- 1 teaspoon vanilla extract

Required Equipment:

- Medium saucepan
- Mixing bowls (1 medium, 1 large)
- Electric mixer or whisk
- Rubber spatula
- Serving dishes or glasses

Preparation:

1. Place the chocolate chips and 1/2 cup of heavy cream in a medium saucepan over low heat. Stir continuously until the chocolate has completely melted and the mixture is smooth. Remove from heat and let it cool to room temperature.

2. In a large mixing bowl, combine the remaining 1 1/2 cups of heavy cream, granulated sugar, and vanilla extract. Use an electric mixer or whisk to beat the mixture until stiff peaks form, indicating that it has reached whipped cream consistency.

3. Take a quarter of the whipped cream and gently fold it into the cooled chocolate mixture using a rubber spatula. This step is crucial for lightening the chocolate mixture before combining it with the rest of the whipped cream.

4. Gently fold in the remaining whipped cream with the chocolate mixture until well combined and no white streaks remain. Be careful not to overmix, as the mousse should be light and airy.

5. Spoon the chocolate mousse into serving dishes or glasses. Chill in the refrigerator for at least 1 hour before serving to allow the mousse to set.

Chef's Tip:

- For an elegant touch, garnish the chocolate mousse with a dollop of whipped cream, chocolate shavings, or fresh berries before serving.
- If you prefer a deeper chocolate flavor, you can use bittersweet chocolate instead of semi-sweet chocolate chips.
- Ensure the chocolate mixture is cool before folding it into the whipped cream to prevent the mousse from becoming too runny.

Nutritional Information per Serving:

- Calories: 520
- Fat: 40g
- Saturated Fat: 25g
- Cholesterol: 120mg
- Sodium: 35mg
- Carbohydrates: 40g
- Fiber: 2g
- Sugar: 35g
- Protein: 4g

Peanut Butter Fudge

Difficulty Level: ★☆☆☆☆

Total Time: 3 hours 15 minutes

Servings: 16 pieces

Ingredients:

- 1 cup creamy peanut butter

- 1/2 cup unsalted butter
- 1/2 teaspoon vanilla extract
- 1/4 teaspoon salt (omit if using salted peanut butter)
- 1 pound powdered sugar (about 3 1/2 to 4 cups, sifted)

Required Equipment:

- 8x8 inch baking dish
- Parchment paper
- Medium saucepan
- Wooden spoon
- Measuring cups and spoons
- Sifter

Preparation:

1. Line the 8x8 inch baking dish with parchment paper, leaving an overhang on two sides to easily lift the fudge out once set.

2. In a medium saucepan, combine the peanut butter and unsalted butter. Heat over medium heat, stirring constantly, until both are completely melted and well combined.

3. Remove the saucepan from the heat. Stir in the vanilla extract and salt until evenly distributed.

4. Gradually add the sifted powdered sugar to the peanut butter mixture, stirring continuously until the mixture becomes thick and smooth.

5. Transfer the fudge mixture to the prepared baking dish. Use the back of the wooden spoon or a spatula to spread the fudge evenly into the dish.

6. Refrigerate the fudge for at least 3 hours, or until it is firm and set.

7. Once set, use the parchment paper overhangs to lift the fudge out of the dish. Place it on a cutting board and cut into 16 equal pieces.

Chef's Tip:

- For a fun twist, sprinkle the top of the fudge with crushed peanuts or mini chocolate chips before refrigerating.
- If the fudge mixture is too stiff to spread easily, lightly dampen your hands with water and press it into the dish.
- Store leftover fudge in an airtight container in the refrigerator for up to 2 weeks.

Nutritional Information per Serving:

- Calories: 280
- Fat: 16g
- Saturated Fat: 7g
- Cholesterol: 15mg
- Sodium: 95mg
- Carbohydrates: 34g
- Fiber: 1g
- Sugar: 32g
- Protein: 4g

Tiramisu

Difficulty Level: ★★☆☆☆

Total Time: 4 hours 30 minutes

Servings: 8

Ingredients:

- 6 large egg yolks
- 3/4 cup granulated sugar
- 1 cup mascarpone cheese, softened
- 1 1/2 cups heavy cream
- 2 cups strong brewed coffee, cooled
- 1/2 cup coffee liqueur (optional)
- 1 package (7 ounces) ladyfingers
- Cocoa powder, for dusting
- Dark chocolate shavings, for garnish

Required Equipment:

- Medium mixing bowl
- Electric mixer
- Whisk
- 9x13 inch dish
- Sifter or fine mesh strainer

Preparation:

1. In a medium mixing bowl, whisk together egg yolks and granulated sugar until well blended and creamy.

2. Add the softened mascarpone cheese to the egg yolk mixture. Use an electric mixer to beat together until smooth and well combined.

3. In a separate mixing bowl, beat the heavy cream with an electric mixer until stiff peaks form.

4. Gently fold the whipped cream into the mascarpone mixture until just combined, being careful not to deflate the cream.

5. In a shallow dish, combine the cooled brewed coffee and coffee liqueur (if using).

6. Quickly dip each ladyfinger into the coffee mixture, making sure not to soak them too long. Arrange a layer of dipped ladyfingers at the bottom of the 9x13 inch dish.

7. Spread half of the mascarpone mixture over the ladyfingers in an even layer.

8. Add another layer of dipped ladyfingers on top of the mascarpone layer.

9. Spread the remaining mascarpone mixture over the second layer of ladyfingers.

10. Cover and refrigerate for at least 4 hours, or overnight, to allow the tiramisu to set.

11. Before serving, dust the top of the tiramisu with cocoa powder and garnish with dark chocolate shavings.

Chef's Tip:

- For a non-alcoholic version, simply omit the coffee liqueur and use only brewed coffee.

- Ensure the ladyfingers are dipped quickly into the coffee mixture to prevent them from becoming too soggy.

- For a decorative touch, you can pipe the top layer of mascarpone cream with a piping bag and star tip before dusting with cocoa powder.

Nutritional Information per Serving:

- Calories: 490

- Fat: 30g

- Saturated Fat: 18g

- Cholesterol: 245mg

- Sodium: 95mg

- Carbohydrates: 44g

- Sugar: 33g

- Protein: 7g

Banana Split Parfaits

Difficulty Level: ★★☆☆☆ (Easy)

Ingredients:

- 2 bananas (sliced)

- 1 cup vanilla yogurt
- 1/4 cup chocolate syrup
- 1/4 cup chopped nuts
- 1/4 cup whipped cream
- 4 maraschino cherries

Instructions:

1. In 4 small glasses, layer sliced bananas and vanilla yogurt.
2. Drizzle each with chocolate syrup.
3. Top with whipped cream, sprinkle with nuts, and add a cherry on top.

Nutritional Information (per parfait):

- Calories: 210
- Protein: 5g
- Carbohydrates: 34g
- Fat: 7g

Mini Fruit Tarts

Difficulty Level: ★★★☆☆ (Moderate)

Ingredients:

- 6 pre-made tart shells
- 1/2 cup vanilla pudding
- 1/4 cup sliced strawberries
- 1/4 cup blueberries
- 1/4 cup kiwi (diced)
- 1 teaspoon honey (optional)

Instructions:

1. Fill each tart shell with vanilla pudding.
2. Arrange the fruit on top in a decorative pattern.
3. Drizzle with honey if desired. Chill before serving.

Nutritional Information (per tart):

- Calories: 180
- Protein: 3g
- Carbohydrates: 22g
- Fat: 9g

Coconut Macaroons

Difficulty Level: ★★★☆☆ (Moderate)

Ingredients:

- 2 cups shredded coconut
- 1/4 cup sweetened condensed milk
- 1 teaspoon vanilla extract
- 2 egg whites
- 1/4 teaspoon salt

Instructions:

1. Preheat oven to 325°F (160°C). Line a baking sheet with parchment paper.
2. In a bowl, mix shredded coconut, sweetened condensed milk, and vanilla extract.
3. In another bowl, beat egg whites with salt until stiff peaks form. Fold into the coconut mixture.
4. Drop spoonfuls onto the baking sheet and bake for 20-25 minutes, or until golden brown.

Nutritional Information (per macaroon):

- Calories: 100
- Protein: 2g
- Carbohydrates: 11g
- Fat: 6g

Chocolate-Covered Strawberries

Difficulty Level: ★★☆☆☆ (Easy)

Ingredients:

- 12 fresh strawberries
- 1/2 cup dark chocolate chips
- 1 tablespoon coconut oil

Instructions:

1. Wash and dry strawberries thoroughly.
2. Melt chocolate chips with coconut oil in the microwave, stirring until smooth.
3. Dip each strawberry into the chocolate and place on a parchment-lined tray.
4. Chill in the refrigerator for 15 minutes until the chocolate hardens.

Nutritional Information (per strawberry):

- Calories: 45
- Protein: 0.5g
- Carbohydrates: 4g
- Fat: 3g

No-Bake Oreo Cheesecake Cups

Difficulty Level: ★★☆☆☆ (Easy)

Ingredients:

- 8 Oreo cookies (crushed)
- 1 cup cream cheese (softened)
- 1/2 cup whipped cream
- 1/4 cup powdered sugar
- 1/2 teaspoon vanilla extract

Instructions:

1. Divide half of the crushed Oreos into 4 small cups.
2. In a bowl, mix cream cheese, whipped cream, powdered sugar, and vanilla until smooth.
3. Spoon the mixture into the cups over the Oreos.
4. Top with the remaining crushed Oreos and chill for at least 30 minutes before serving.

Nutritional Information (per cup):

- Calories: 250
- Protein: 3g
- Carbohydrates: 24g
- Fat: 16g

Chapter 7: Smoothies and Drinks Recipes

Strawberry Banana Smoothie

Difficulty Level: ★☆☆☆☆

Total Time: 5 minutes

Servings: 2

Ingredients:

- 1 ripe banana, sliced
- 1 cup fresh strawberries, hulled
- 1/2 cup Greek yogurt
- 1 cup milk (any variety)
- 1 tablespoon honey (optional)
- Ice cubes (optional)

Required Equipment:

- Blender
- Measuring cups and spoons
- Knife
- Cutting board

Preparation:

1. Place the sliced banana and hulled strawberries into the blender.

2. Add the Greek yogurt and milk to the blender.

3. If desired, add 1 tablespoon of honey for extra sweetness.

4. For a colder smoothie, add a handful of ice cubes to the blender.

5. Blend on high speed until all the ingredients are smooth and well combined, about 1-2 minutes.

6. Pour the smoothie into two glasses and serve immediately.

Chef's Tip:

- For a vegan version, use plant-based milk and yogurt. Agave syrup can be used as a substitute for honey.

- To make the smoothie thicker, add more banana or use frozen strawberries instead of fresh.

- Add a scoop of protein powder to turn this smoothie into a filling breakfast or post-workout snack.

Nutritional Information per Serving:

- Calories: 180
- Fat: 2g
- Saturated Fat: 1g
- Cholesterol: 5mg
- Sodium: 60mg
- Carbohydrates: 34g
- Fiber: 4g
- Sugar: 24g
- Protein: 8g

Mango Pineapple Smoothie

Difficulty Level: ★☆☆☆☆

Total Time: 5 minutes

Servings: 2

Ingredients:

- 1 cup frozen mango chunks
- 1 cup frozen pineapple chunks
- 1 banana, sliced
- 1 cup orange juice
- 1/2 cup vanilla yogurt
- Fresh mint leaves (for garnish, optional)

Required Equipment:

- Blender
- Measuring cups
- Knife
- Serving glasses

Preparation:

1. Place the frozen mango chunks, frozen pineapple chunks, and sliced banana into the blender.

2. Pour the orange juice over the fruit in the blender.

3. Add the vanilla yogurt to the blender.

4. Blend on high speed until the mixture is smooth and creamy, about 1-2 minutes. If the smoothie is too thick, you can add a little more orange juice to reach your desired consistency.

5. Pour the smoothie into serving glasses.

6. Garnish with fresh mint leaves, if desired, and serve immediately.

Chef's Tip:

- For an extra boost of nutrition, add a tablespoon of flaxseed or chia seeds to the smoothie before blending.

- If you prefer your smoothies a bit colder, you can add a few ice cubes to the blender along with the other ingredients.

- To make this smoothie vegan, ensure the vanilla yogurt used is dairy-free.

Nutritional Information per Serving:

- Calories: 210
- Fat: 1g
- Saturated Fat: 0.5g
- Cholesterol: 3mg
- Sodium: 20mg
- Carbohydrates: 50g
- Fiber: 4g
- Sugar: 36g
- Protein: 4g

Green Detox Smoothie

Difficulty Level: ★☆☆☆☆

Total Time: 10 minutes

Servings: 2

Ingredients:

- 1 cup spinach leaves, tightly packed
- 1 small cucumber, peeled and chopped

- 1 medium green apple, cored and sliced
- 1 ripe banana, peeled and sliced
- 1/2 cup fresh pineapple chunks
- 1 tablespoon chia seeds
- 1 cup coconut water or plain water
- Ice cubes (optional)

Required Equipment:

- Blender
- Measuring cups and spoons
- Knife
- Cutting board

Preparation:

1. Prepare all the fruits and vegetables by washing them thoroughly. Peel the cucumber, core the apple, and slice the banana. Chop the cucumber and apple into smaller pieces to make blending easier.

2. Add the spinach leaves to the blender first. This helps in blending the leaves more efficiently when the liquid is added.

3. Add the chopped cucumber, apple slices, banana slices, and pineapple chunks on top of the spinach.

4. Sprinkle the tablespoon of chia seeds over the fruits and vegetables.

5. Pour 1 cup of coconut water or plain water into the blender. If you prefer a colder smoothie, add a few ice cubes as well.

6. Blend on high speed until all the ingredients are thoroughly combined and the smoothie reaches your desired consistency. If the smoothie is too thick, you can add a little more water to thin it out.

7. Taste the smoothie and adjust the sweetness if necessary. Depending on the ripeness of the fruits, you might want to add a teaspoon of honey or maple syrup.

8. Once blended to perfection, pour the smoothie into two glasses and serve immediately.

Chef's Tip:

- For an extra boost of nutrition, you can add a scoop of your favorite protein powder or a handful of nuts like almonds or walnuts into the smoothie before blending.
- If you're making this smoothie ahead of time, store it in an airtight container in the refrigerator for up to 24 hours. Shake well before serving as the ingredients may settle.

- Customize your detox smoothie by adding other green vegetables like kale or avocado for added creaminess and nutrients.

Nutritional Information per Serving:

- Calories: 180
- Fat: 2g
- Saturated Fat: 0g
- Cholesterol: 0mg
- Sodium: 60mg
- Carbohydrates: 40g
- Fiber: 8g
- Sugar: 25g
- Protein: 3g

Chocolate Peanut Butter Smoothie

Difficulty Level: ★☆☆☆☆

Total Time: 5 minutes

Servings: 2

Ingredients:

- 2 bananas, frozen
- 2 tablespoons creamy peanut butter
- 2 tablespoons cocoa powder
- 1 cup milk (any kind)
- 1 tablespoon honey, or to taste
- Ice cubes (optional)

Required Equipment:

- Blender
- Measuring spoons
- Measuring cup
- Serving glasses

Preparation:

1. Place the frozen bananas, creamy peanut butter, cocoa powder, milk, and honey into the blender.

2. Blend on high speed until the mixture is smooth and creamy. If the smoothie is too thick, you can add a little more milk to reach your desired consistency.

3. Taste the smoothie and adjust the sweetness by adding more honey if needed.

4. If you prefer a colder smoothie, add a few ice cubes and blend again until smooth.

5. Pour the smoothie into serving glasses.

Chef's Tip:

- For a vegan version, use almond milk or any other plant-based milk and ensure the cocoa powder and peanut butter are vegan-friendly.

- Add a scoop of protein powder for an extra protein boost, making it a great post-workout snack.

- Garnish with a sprinkle of cocoa powder or a few slices of banana for an appealing presentation.

Nutritional Information per Serving:

- Calories: 280
- Fat: 10g
- Saturated Fat: 2g
- Cholesterol: 5mg
- Sodium: 150mg
- Carbohydrates: 44g
- Fiber: 6g
- Sugar: 28g
- Protein: 8g

Blueberry Almond Smoothie

Difficulty Level: ★☆☆☆☆

Total Time: 5 minutes

Servings: 2

Ingredients:

- 1 cup fresh blueberries
- 1 banana, sliced
- 1/2 cup unsweetened almond milk
- 1/2 cup Greek yogurt
- 2 tablespoons almond butter
- 1 tablespoon honey (optional)

- Ice cubes (optional)

Required Equipment:

- Blender
- Measuring cups and spoons
- Serving glasses

Preparation:

1. Place the fresh blueberries, sliced banana, unsweetened almond milk, Greek yogurt, and almond butter into the blender.
2. Add honey to taste if you prefer a sweeter smoothie. This step is optional.
3. If you like your smoothie colder and thicker, add a handful of ice cubes.
4. Blend on high speed until the mixture is smooth and creamy, usually about 1-2 minutes.
5. Pour the smoothie into serving glasses.
6. Serve immediately for the best taste and texture.

Chef's Tip:

- For an extra protein boost, you can add a scoop of your favorite vanilla or unflavored protein powder to the blender before mixing.
- If the smoothie is too thick for your liking, add a little more almond milk until you reach your desired consistency.
- To make this smoothie ahead of time, prepare the ingredients in the blender jar, cover, and store in the refrigerator overnight. Blend in the morning for a quick and nutritious breakfast.

Nutritional Information per Serving:

- Calories: 280
- Fat: 15g
- Saturated Fat: 2g
- Cholesterol: 5mg
- Sodium: 80mg
- Carbohydrates: 30g
- Fiber: 5g
- Sugar: 18g (varies with the use of honey)
- Protein: 10g

Tropical Coconut Smoothie

Difficulty Level: ★☆☆☆☆

Total Time: 10 minutes

Servings: 2

Ingredients:

- 1 cup coconut milk
- 1 banana, sliced and frozen
- 1/2 cup pineapple chunks, frozen
- 1/2 cup mango chunks, frozen
- 2 tablespoons shredded coconut
- 1 tablespoon honey (optional)
- Ice cubes (optional, adjust based on desired thickness)

Required Equipment:

- Blender
- Measuring cups and spoons
- Serving glasses

Preparation:

1. Pour 1 cup of coconut milk into the blender.
2. Add the sliced and frozen banana to the blender.
3. Include 1/2 cup of frozen pineapple chunks and 1/2 cup of frozen mango chunks.
4. Sprinkle 2 tablespoons of shredded coconut into the mixture.
5. If desired, add 1 tablespoon of honey for extra sweetness.
6. For a thicker smoothie, add a few ice cubes to the blender.
7. Blend all ingredients on high speed until smooth and creamy, approximately 1-2 minutes.
8. Pour the smoothie into serving glasses.
9. Optionally, garnish with a sprinkle of shredded coconut or a slice of pineapple on the rim of the glass for decoration.

Chef's Tip:

- For an extra tropical twist, add a splash of pineapple juice or a few drops of coconut extract to enhance the flavors.
- If the smoothie is too thick, add more coconut milk a little at a time until the desired consistency is reached.
- To make this smoothie vegan-friendly, ensure the honey is substituted with agave syrup or simply omit it.

Nutritional Information per Serving:

- Calories: 250
- Fat: 14g
- Saturated Fat: 12g
- Sodium: 20mg
- Carbohydrates: 30g
- Fiber: 3g
- Sugar: 20g (varies if honey is added)
- Protein: 2g

Raspberry Lemonade

Difficulty Level: ★☆☆☆☆

Total Time: 15 minutes

Servings: 4

Ingredients:

- 1 cup fresh raspberries
- 3/4 cup granulated sugar
- 1 cup water
- 3/4 cup freshly squeezed lemon juice (about 4-5 lemons)
- 4 cups cold water
- Ice cubes
- Additional raspberries and lemon slices for garnish

Required Equipment:

- Saucepan
- Fine mesh strainer
- Pitcher
- Wooden spoon
- Juicer (optional)

Preparation:

1. In a saucepan over medium heat, combine 1 cup of fresh raspberries, 3/4 cup of granulated sugar, and 1 cup of water. Stir continuously until the sugar has dissolved and the mixture comes to a simmer. Remove from heat and allow to cool slightly.

2. Pour the raspberry mixture through a fine mesh strainer into a pitcher, pressing on the solids with a wooden spoon to extract as much liquid as possible. Discard the solids.

3. Add 3/4 cup of freshly squeezed lemon juice to the pitcher with the raspberry syrup. Stir to combine.

4. Stir in 4 cups of cold water. Taste and adjust sweetness by adding more sugar if desired, stirring until dissolved.

5. Add ice cubes to the pitcher and stir until the lemonade is chilled.

6. Serve the raspberry lemonade over ice, garnished with additional raspberries and lemon slices.

Chef's Tip:

- For an extra refreshing twist, add a few mint leaves to the raspberry mixture while simmering. Remove the leaves when straining the mixture.
- If the lemonade is too tart or too sweet for your taste, adjust the amount of lemon juice or sugar accordingly.
- To make a fizzy raspberry lemonade, replace 1 cup of the cold water with 1 cup of sparkling water. Add the sparkling water just before serving to maintain its fizz.

Nutritional Information per Serving:

- Calories: 180
- Fat: 0g
- Saturated Fat: 0g
- Cholesterol: 0mg
- Sodium: 10mg
- Carbohydrates: 46g
- Fiber: 2g
- Sugar: 42g
- Protein: 1g

Iced Matcha Latte

Difficulty Level: ★☆☆☆☆

Total Time: 10 minutes

Servings: 2

Ingredients:

- 2 teaspoons matcha green tea powder
- 2 tablespoons hot water (not boiling)
- 1 1/2 cups cold milk (any variety)
- 1-2 tablespoons honey or sugar (adjust to taste)
- Ice cubes
- Optional: whipped cream, for topping

Required Equipment:

- Bowl
- Whisk
- Measuring spoons
- Glasses

Preparation:

1. In a bowl, add 2 teaspoons of matcha green tea powder.

2. Pour 2 tablespoons of hot water over the matcha powder. Whisk vigorously until the matcha is fully dissolved and there are no lumps, creating a smooth paste.

3. In a separate glass, fill it with ice cubes to your preference.

4. Pour the matcha paste over the ice.

5. Add 1 1/2 cups of cold milk to the glass. Stir in 1-2 tablespoons of honey or sugar, adjusting the sweetness to your taste.

6. Stir well until the matcha mixture and milk are fully combined.

7. If desired, top with whipped cream for an extra treat.

8. Serve immediately and enjoy your refreshing Iced Matcha Latte.

Chef's Tip:

- For a frothier latte, you can shake the matcha paste, milk, and sweetener together in a sealed jar before pouring it over ice.
- Experiment with different types of milk to find your preferred taste and texture. Almond, coconut, and oat milk are great dairy-free options.

- To enhance the matcha flavor, try adding a few drops of vanilla extract to the mixture.

Nutritional Information per Serving:

- Calories: 120 (varies depending on milk and sweetener used)
- Fat: 3g (varies depending on milk used)
- Carbohydrates: 20g (varies depending on sweetener used)
- Protein: 8g (varies depending on milk used)
- Sugar: 18g (varies depending on sweetener used)

Watermelon Mint Cooler

Difficulty Level: ★☆☆☆☆

Total Time: 10 minutes

Servings: 2

Ingredients:

- 4 cups cubed seedless watermelon
- 1/2 cup fresh mint leaves, plus more for garnish
- 2 tablespoons lime juice
- 2 tablespoons honey (optional)
- 1 cup ice cubes
- Sparkling water (optional, for serving)

Required Equipment:

- Blender
- Measuring cups and spoons
- Knife
- Cutting board
- Serving glasses

Preparation:

1. Place the cubed watermelon, fresh mint leaves, lime juice, and honey (if using) into the blender.
2. Add the ice cubes to the blender.
3. Blend on high speed until the mixture is smooth and the ice is completely crushed.
4. Taste the cooler and adjust sweetness with additional honey if desired.

5. If a thinner consistency is preferred, blend in a splash of sparkling water until the desired consistency is reached.

6. Pour the watermelon mint cooler into serving glasses.

7. Garnish each glass with a sprig of fresh mint.

8. Serve immediately for a refreshing drink.

Chef's Tip:

- For an extra chill, freeze the watermelon cubes before blending. This will make the cooler even more refreshing and reduce the need for ice, resulting in a more concentrated flavor.

- To turn this cooler into a festive drink, add a splash of coconut water or a non-alcoholic sparkling beverage before serving.

- For an adult version, a shot of rum or vodka can be blended in with the other ingredients.

Nutritional Information per Serving:

- Calories: 100
- Fat: 0g
- Saturated Fat: 0g
- Cholesterol: 0mg
- Sodium: 5mg
- Carbohydrates: 25g
- Fiber: 1g
- Sugar: 20g (varies with the use of honey)
- Protein: 1g

Peach Iced Tea

Difficulty Level: ★☆☆☆☆

Total Time: 15 minutes

Servings: 4

Ingredients:

- 4 black tea bags
- 4 cups boiling water
- 1/3 cup honey or sugar (adjust to taste)
- 2 ripe peaches, pitted and sliced
- Ice cubes, for serving

- Fresh mint leaves, for garnish (optional)

Required Equipment:

- Teapot or large heatproof pitcher
- Measuring cups and spoons
- Knife
- Cutting board
- Spoon for stirring
- Serving glasses

Preparation:

1. Place the tea bags in a teapot or large heatproof pitcher.

2. Pour 4 cups of boiling water over the tea bags. Allow the tea to steep for 5 minutes.

3. While the tea is steeping, prepare the peaches by pitting and slicing them on a cutting board.

4. Remove the tea bags from the pitcher after steeping and discard them.

5. Stir in 1/3 cup of honey or sugar into the hot tea until fully dissolved. Adjust the sweetness according to your preference.

6. Add the sliced peaches to the tea and let it cool to room temperature.

7. Once cooled, refrigerate the peach tea until chilled, about 1 hour.

8. To serve, fill glasses with ice cubes and pour the chilled peach tea over the ice. Garnish with fresh mint leaves if desired.

Chef's Tip:

- For a stronger peach flavor, puree one of the peaches and stir the puree into the tea before chilling.

- If you prefer a clearer tea, you can strain the tea to remove the peach slices before serving, or leave them in for added flavor and presentation.

- Experiment with different sweeteners like maple syrup or agave nectar for a unique twist on this refreshing drink.

Nutritional Information per Serving:

- Calories: 100 (varies depending on the amount and type of sweetener used)
- Fat: 0g
- Sodium: 10mg
- Carbohydrates: 26g
- Fiber: 1g
- Sugar: 25g (varies depending on the amount and type of sweetener used)
- Protein: 1g

Cherry Vanilla Smoothie

Difficulty Level: ★☆☆☆☆ (Very Easy)

Ingredients:

- 1 cup frozen cherries
- 1/2 cup vanilla yogurt
- 1/2 cup almond milk
- 1 teaspoon honey (optional)
- 1/2 teaspoon vanilla extract

Instructions:

1. Add cherries, yogurt, almond milk, honey, and vanilla extract to a blender.
2. Blend until smooth and creamy.
3. Pour into a glass and serve immediately.

Nutritional Information (per serving):

- Calories: 180
- Protein: 5g
- Carbohydrates: 33g
- Fat: 2g

Cucumber Lime Refresher

Difficulty Level: ★☆☆☆☆ (Very Easy)

Ingredients:

- 1 cucumber (sliced)
- 1 lime (juiced)
- 2 cups water
- 1 teaspoon honey (optional)
- Ice cubes

Instructions:

1. Add cucumber slices, lime juice, and honey to a pitcher of water.
2. Stir well and let it sit for 10 minutes.
3. Pour into glasses over ice and serve.

Nutritional Information (per serving):

- Calories: 20
- Protein: 0g
- Carbohydrates: 5g

- Fat: 0g

Avocado and Spinach Smoothie

Difficulty Level: ★★☆☆☆ (Easy)

Ingredients:

- 1/2 avocado
- 1 cup spinach
- 1/2 banana
- 1 cup coconut water
- 1 teaspoon chia seeds

Instructions:

1. Combine avocado, spinach, banana, coconut water, and chia seeds in a blender.
2. Blend until smooth and creamy.
3. Pour into a glass and enjoy immediately.

Nutritional Information (per serving):

- Calories: 210
- Protein: 3g
- Carbohydrates: 25g
- Fat: 10g

Orange Carrot Ginger Juice

Difficulty Level: ★★☆☆☆ (Easy)

Ingredients:

- 2 oranges (peeled)
- 2 carrots (peeled and chopped)
- 1/2 inch piece of fresh ginger
- 1 cup water
- Ice cubes

Instructions:

1. Add oranges, carrots, ginger, and water to a blender.

2. Blend until smooth. Strain the juice through a fine mesh sieve if desired.
3. Serve over ice and enjoy.

Nutritional Information (per serving):

- Calories: 120
- Protein: 2g
- Carbohydrates: 30g
- Fat: 0g

Chocolate Mint Smoothie

Difficulty Level: ★★☆☆☆ (Easy)

Ingredients:

- 1 cup unsweetened almond milk
- 1 frozen banana
- 1 tablespoon cocoa powder
- 1/4 teaspoon peppermint extract
- 1 teaspoon honey (optional)

Instructions:

1. Add almond milk, banana, cocoa powder, peppermint extract, and honey to a blender.
2. Blend until smooth and creamy.
3. Pour into a glass and garnish with a sprig of fresh mint if desired.

Nutritional Information (per serving):

- Calories: 160
- Protein: 2g
- Carbohydrates: 30g
- Fat: 4g

Chapter 8: Advanced Cooking Techniques

Experimenting with Flavors

The art of cooking is as much about creativity as it is about technique. As you become more comfortable in the kitchen, experimenting with flavors will not only broaden your culinary skills but also enhance your enjoyment of cooking. Here are some advanced techniques to help you explore and master the world of flavors.

1. Understanding Flavor Profiles: Begin by familiarizing yourself with the basic flavor profiles: sweet, salty, sour, bitter, and umami. Each of these plays a crucial role in how we experience food. For instance, sweetness can balance acidity, while umami can add depth to dishes. Experiment by adding a pinch of salt to sweet dishes or a squeeze of lemon to savory dishes to see how it changes the flavor.

2. Using Herbs and Spices: Herbs and spices are the easiest way to add new dimensions to your food. Start with familiar ones like basil, oregano, cumin, and cinnamon, then gradually introduce more exotic flavors such as lemongrass, cardamom, or saffron. Remember, dried herbs and spices have a more concentrated flavor than fresh, so adjust quantities accordingly.

3. Balancing Flavors: Achieving a harmonious balance between the different flavor profiles is key to creating dishes that are pleasing to the palate. If a dish is too acidic, add a sweet component. If it's overly sweet, a bit of acid or bitterness can provide balance. Practice this by tasting your food as you cook and adjusting the flavors as needed.

4. Layering Flavors: Building layers of flavor can transform a simple dish into something complex and intriguing. This can be achieved by marinating proteins, toasting spices before cooking, or deglazing a pan to incorporate the browned bits into a sauce. Each step adds a new layer, contributing to the overall depth of the dish.

5. Pairing Flavors: Some flavors naturally complement each other, while others can create a striking contrast that elevates the dish. Explore classic pairings like tomato and basil, pork and apple, or chocolate and orange. Then, venture into more adventurous combinations, such as watermelon and feta or chili and chocolate, to discover new favorites.

6. Experimenting with Texture: Flavor isn't just about taste; texture plays a significant role in how we enjoy food. Incorporating elements with contrasting textures, like adding crunchy nuts to a smooth soup or crispy toppings to creamy desserts, can make a dish more interesting and satisfying.

7. Cooking Methods: Different cooking methods can bring out unique flavors and textures in ingredients. Roasting vegetables caramelizes their natural sugars, enhancing their sweetness, while slow cooking meat breaks down its fibers, making it tender and rich in flavor. Experiment with various techniques to find what works best for each ingredient.

8. Seasonal and Fresh Ingredients: Fresh, seasonal ingredients often offer the best flavors. They require less manipulation to shine in a dish. Visit local farmers' markets to inspire your cooking and experiment with ingredients at their peak of freshness.

9. Tasting and Adjusting: The most important technique in experimenting with flavors is tasting your food as you cook. Your palate will guide you in making adjustments, whether it's adding a bit more salt, a splash of vinegar, or a sprinkle of sugar, to achieve the perfect balance.

By embracing these techniques, you'll not only expand your culinary repertoire but also develop a deeper appreciation for the art of cooking. Remember, the key to mastering flavors lies in experimentation, so don't be afraid to try new combinations and techniques. With practice, you'll be able to create dishes that are not only delicious but also a true reflection of your creativity and passion for cooking.

Mastering the Art of Presentation

Once you've honed your skills in **experimenting with flavors,** the next step in your culinary journey is to master the art of presentation. The way your dish looks can be just as important as how it tastes, especially when you're aiming to impress friends and family or share your creations on social media. Here are some key techniques to elevate the visual appeal of your dishes:

1. Color Contrast: Use ingredients with different colors to create a visually appealing plate. Bright vegetables like bell peppers, green beans, or cherry tomatoes can add a pop of color to more neutral dishes. Think about how the colors on your plate complement each other to make your dish stand out.

2. Plate Selection: The plate is your canvas, so choose wisely. White plates are classic as they make the colors of the food pop, but don't be afraid to experiment with different shapes and colors. Just ensure the plate complements the food and doesn't distract from it.

3. Composition: Balance and composition are key. Start by placing your main ingredient on the plate, then add your sides or garnishes around it in a way that is pleasing to the eye. Odd numbers are visually more appealing, so consider placing three or five components on the plate rather than even numbers.

4. Height: Building height on your plate can add an element of sophistication. Stack ingredients or use tools like ring molds to create layers. This not only adds visual interest but can also make a simple dish look more complex and thoughtfully prepared.

5. Garnishes: A well-chosen garnish can enhance both the flavor and appearance of your dish. Fresh herbs, edible flowers, or a sprinkle of seeds can add texture and color. Remember, the garnish should be edible and complement the overall dish.

6. Sauce Art: Sauces offer a great opportunity to add flair to your presentation. Instead of pouring the sauce over the dish, try using a spoon or squeeze bottle to create designs on the plate. A simple zigzag or a few dots can turn an ordinary dish into a work of art.

7. Negative Space: Don't feel the need to fill every inch of the plate. Leaving some negative space can make your dish look more elegant and deliberate. Think of it as framing your creation, allowing each component to stand out.

8. Texture: Similar to flavor layering, incorporating different textures can make a dish more visually interesting. A combination of smooth and crunchy elements, for example, can add depth to your presentation.

9. Precision: Take your time to carefully place each element on the plate. Use tools like tweezers for small garnishes to ensure every component is precisely where you want it. This attention to detail can make a big difference in the final presentation.

By focusing on these aspects of presentation, you'll not only enhance the visual appeal of your dishes but also the overall dining experience. Remember, people eat with their eyes first, so taking the time to present your food beautifully can make it even more enjoyable to eat. Whether you're cooking for yourself, your family, or sharing your creations online, mastering the art of presentation is a valuable skill that will take your culinary creations to the next level.

Experimenting with Flavors

10. Embracing Regional and International Flavors: One of the most exciting aspects of cooking is the opportunity to explore and incorporate flavors from around the world. Start by selecting a region or country that interests you and research traditional spices, herbs, and cooking techniques used in that cuisine. For example, if you're intrigued by Italian cooking, you might experiment with basil, oregano, and olive oil in your dishes. Or, if you're drawn to Thai cuisine, you could explore the use of lemongrass, galangal, and fish sauce. This not only broadens your culinary horizons but also introduces you to a world of new flavors and combinations.

11. Infusing Flavors: Infusions are a fantastic way to impart subtle flavors into oils, syrups, and even water. By gently heating your base with aromatic ingredients like herbs, spices, or citrus peels, you allow their flavors to meld and create a new, infused ingredient that can add a unique twist to your dishes. For instance, rosemary-infused olive oil can add a Mediterranean flair to your salads, while vanilla-infused syrup can elevate your homemade desserts.

12. The Role of Acidity and Sweetness: Acidity and sweetness are powerful tools in balancing flavors. Adding a touch of vinegar or lemon juice can brighten a dish and cut through richness, while a hint of sugar or honey can mellow out overly acidic or spicy flavors. Experiment with adding these elements in small increments to find the perfect balance that suits your taste.

13. Experimenting with Salts: Not all salts are created equal. Beyond the common table salt, there's a whole world of gourmet salts to explore, each with its own unique flavor profile and texture. Himalayan pink salt, for example, can add a crunchy texture and a mild flavor, while smoked sea salt can introduce a subtle smokiness to your dishes. Experimenting with different salts can add an unexpected twist to your cooking.

14. The Magic of Marinades: Marinades not only tenderize meats but also infuse them with flavor. By combining acids (like vinegar or citrus juice), oils, and a variety of herbs and spices, you can create a marinade that transforms the taste and texture of your proteins. Don't be afraid to experiment with different marinade ingredients to discover combinations that you love.

15. Creative Condiments: Sometimes, the right condiment can turn a good dish into a great one. Experiment with making your own condiments, such as homemade ketchup, mustard, or mayonnaise, and customize them with unique ingredients to suit your taste. For example, adding chipotle peppers to mayonnaise can give it a smoky, spicy kick that's perfect for sandwiches and burgers.

16. The Importance of Freshness: The freshness of your ingredients can significantly impact the flavor of your dishes. Whenever possible, use fresh herbs, spices, and produce. Fresh herbs, for instance, have a brighter, more vibrant flavor than their dried counterparts and can make a big difference in the final taste of your dish.

17. Experimenting with Sweet and Savory: Don't be afraid to mix sweet and savory elements in your cooking. The contrast between the two can create complex, intriguing flavors that surprise and delight the palate. For example, adding a touch of honey to a savory dish like roasted carrots can enhance their natural sweetness, while a sprinkle of sea salt on dark chocolate can intensify its rich, bitter notes.

18. Textural Contrasts: Just as with flavor, contrasting textures can make a dish more interesting and enjoyable to eat. Consider combining creamy elements with crunchy ones, like adding croutons to a smooth soup or nuts to a soft salad. This contrast not only adds variety to the eating experience but also enhances the overall flavor profile of the dish.

Chapter 9: Sharing Your Creations

Once you've mastered the art of cooking and presentation, the next exciting step is to share your culinary creations with the world. Social media platforms like Instagram and TikTok have become vibrant spaces for young chefs to showcase their dishes, connect with fellow food enthusiasts, and even gain a following. Here's how you can effectively use **food photography** and **styling tips** to make your dishes stand out online.

1. Lighting is Key: Natural light is your best friend when it comes to food photography. Try to take pictures during the day near a window where you can get plenty of indirect sunlight. This will highlight the textures and colors of your food, making it look more appetizing.

2. The Rule of Thirds: When taking photos, imagine your image is divided into nine equal segments by two vertical and two horizontal lines. Placing the main elements of your dish along these lines or at their intersections can make your photo more balanced and visually appealing.

3. Angles Matter: Different dishes look best from different angles. Overhead shots work great for dishes where you want to showcase the arrangement and components, like a pizza or a salad. Side angles are perfect for showing off layers, like cakes or burgers. Experiment with various angles to find what best highlights the uniqueness of each dish.

4. Pay Attention to Background: Keep the background simple to ensure the focus remains on the food. Neutral colors and textures work best as they don't distract from the dish. A plain white plate or a rustic wooden table can serve as great backdrops.

5. Props and Garnishes: Adding props like cutlery, napkins, or ingredients used in the dish can add context and depth to your photos. However, be careful not to overcrowd the scene. Garnishes should enhance the look of your dish, not hide it. A sprig of fresh herbs or a dusting of powdered sugar can add that final touch.

6. Editing Apps: Use photo editing apps sparingly to enhance your photos. Adjusting the brightness, contrast, and saturation can help make your dishes pop, but avoid over-editing. The goal is to make the food look inviting and true to life.

7. Consistency in Style: Developing a consistent style helps in building a recognizable brand. Whether it's a specific filter, angle, or composition, consistency will make your feed look cohesive and more professional.

8. Engage with Your Audience: Don't just post and forget. Respond to comments, ask for feedback, and engage with other food accounts. Social media is as much about community as it is about showcasing your creations.

9. Use Hashtags and Tags: Utilize relevant hashtags and tag food-related accounts or brands used in your recipe. This can increase the visibility of your posts and help you reach a wider audience.

10. Tell a Story: Behind every dish is a story. Share your inspiration, the recipe, or any tips and tricks you learned while making the dish. This personal touch can make your content more relatable and engaging.

By following these tips, you'll not only be able to share your culinary creations but also inspire others, gain confidence in your cooking and photography skills, and maybe even start building your own brand on social media. Remember, the most important thing is to have fun and let your creativity shine through your dishes and their presentation.

Food Photography for Social Media

When capturing your culinary creations for social media, it's essential to focus on **composition and framing**. This involves carefully arranging the elements of your dish and its surroundings to create a visually appealing image. Start by considering the placement of your main dish, garnishes, and any props you're using. Aim for a balance that draws the eye toward the focal point of your photo, usually the dish itself. Use the **rule of thirds** as a guide, positioning key elements along the lines or at the intersections to achieve a harmonious composition.

Focus and clarity are paramount in food photography. Ensure your dish is the sharpest part of your image, using your camera or phone's focus features. A crisp, clear photo invites viewers to imagine the textures and flavors of your dish, making it more enticing. If your camera allows, experiment with depth of field by keeping your dish in sharp focus while gently blurring the background. This technique can add depth to your photos and make the dish stand out.

Color and texture play significant roles in making your food look appetizing. Vibrant, fresh ingredients naturally look more appealing, so highlight these elements in your photography. Use contrasting colors and textures to create visual interest. For example, the bright red of sliced strawberries on a smooth, creamy cheesecake can add a pop of color that catches the eye. Similarly, the contrast between the crispy golden crust of a pie and its soft, luscious filling can entice viewers.

Editing your photos can enhance their appeal, but it's crucial to keep edits subtle and natural. Adjusting the brightness, contrast, and saturation can help your dish look its best, but avoid over-editing, which can make the food look unnatural. Many social media platforms and photo editing apps offer filters designed to enhance food photos; use these sparingly to maintain the authenticity of your dish.

Consistency in your photography style helps build your brand on social media. Whether it's a particular filter, a consistent color scheme, or a unique angle you shoot from, maintaining a recognizable style can make your content stand out in a crowded feed. This doesn't mean all your photos need to look the same, but a cohesive aesthetic can make your profile more visually appealing and encourage viewers to follow your culinary journey.

Engaging with your audience is as important as the quality of your photos. Include captions that tell the story behind your dish, share cooking tips, or ask your followers for their thoughts and experiences. This interaction can foster a community around your content, increasing engagement and visibility. Regularly responding to comments and messages also builds a connection with your audience, making them more likely to continue following and supporting your culinary adventures.

Hashtags and tagging can significantly increase the reach of your posts. Use relevant hashtags that describe your dish, the ingredients, or the occasion. Tagging the brands of ingredients or equipment you used can also attract attention from those brands and their followers. Research popular food-related hashtags and consider creating a unique hashtag for your content to make it easily discoverable.

Experimentation and learning are key to improving your food photography for social media. Try new techniques, seek inspiration from other food photographers, and don't be afraid to experiment with different styles. Photography, like cooking, is a creative process that evolves over time. With practice and patience, you'll develop a unique visual style that makes your culinary creations shine online.

Styling and Shooting Tips

Crafting the perfect shot for social media involves more than just snapping a quick photo of your latest culinary creation. It requires thoughtfulness in styling and a keen eye for detail to truly make your dishes pop on the screen. One of the most effective ways to enhance the visual appeal of your food photography is through the strategic use of shadows and highlights. Properly placed lighting can create depth and texture, making your dishes look even more enticing. Experiment with different lighting setups to find the one that best accentuates the natural beauty of your food. For instance, side lighting can emphasize the texture of your dish, while backlighting can create a halo effect that makes your food look heavenly.

Another aspect to consider is the balance between the dish and its environment. While the focus should always be on the food, adding elements that tell a story or evoke a certain mood can significantly elevate your photo. For example, a rustic loaf of bread might be photographed on an aged wooden table to suggest warmth and home-cooked comfort. Alternatively, a modern, minimalist dessert could be placed on a sleek, black surface to highlight its sophistication. The key is to choose props and backgrounds that complement the dish without overwhelming it.

When it comes to styling your food, think about the arrangement and how each component interacts with the others. Small adjustments, like wiping away any smudges on the plate or rearranging elements to create a more dynamic composition, can make a big difference. Pay attention to the flow of the dish, guiding the viewer's eye through the photo with lines and shapes that draw attention to the most important parts of the dish. For instance, a drizzle of sauce or a strategically placed sprig of herbs can add movement and interest, leading the eye through the image.

The choice of color palette also plays a crucial role in food photography. Colors can evoke emotions and affect how appetizing the food appears. Warm colors like reds, oranges, and yellows can stimulate appetite, while cool colors like blues and greens can create a refreshing and clean look. Use color theory to your advantage by selecting plates and backgrounds that either contrast or complement the colors of your food, depending on the effect you wish to achieve.

In addition to these styling tips, mastering the technical aspects of your camera or smartphone is essential. Understanding how to control the focus, exposure, and white balance can help you capture the true colors and textures of your dishes. Practice adjusting these settings to see how they affect the final image. For instance, a lower exposure can enhance the moodiness of a photo, while a higher exposure can make it appear light and airy.

Finally, remember that the best food photography tells a story. Whether it's the story of the dish's origin, the process of making it, or the occasion it was made for, incorporating elements that convey this narrative can add depth to your photos. This could be as simple as including the ingredients used in the recipe or as elaborate as setting a scene that reflects the cultural background of the dish. By doing so, you not only capture the attention of your audience but also engage them on a deeper level, inviting them to experience the story behind your culinary creation.

By applying these styling and shooting tips, you'll be well on your way to creating stunning food photographs that stand out on social media. With practice and experimentation, you'll develop your own unique style that reflects your personality and culinary prowess. Remember, the goal is to have fun and express your creativity through your dishes and their presentation, sharing your passion for cooking with the world.

Made in United States
Troutdale, OR
01/08/2025

27766501R00071